The
BATCH
LADY

SUZANNE MULHOLLAND

The BATCH LADY

GRAB AND COOK

EBURY
PRESS

To my husband, Peter, my rock and soulmate, thank you for always being so supportive of what I do, and for always getting everything down from the high shelves for me!

HELLO, AND WELCOME TO MY NEW BOOK!

For those of you who are new to The Batch Lady, welcome. My name is Suzanne Mulholland and let me tell you a secret – I don't like cooking! (Well, not every night, anyway.) For those of you who have followed my journey and bought previous books, thank you for coming back and buying this new one. You already know my secret, and you know that you don't need to love cooking to eat well and put a home-cooked meal on the table.

I've always loved to make meals in advance so that I'm organised for the days or weeks ahead. I want it to be done simply, quickly and with as little fuss as possible. My passion in life is looking at the concepts of 'time' and 'efficiency' . . . how can we tick off all the monotonous day-to-day chores that need to be done well, but in the shortest amount of time? I don't believe anybody wants to spend their days in a cycle of tedium, doing the same chores over and over again – I certainly don't! I'd much rather be laughing with friends, reading a good book, going on a nice dog walk, doing something fun with the kids or simply putting my feet up with a G&T.

So what's Grab and Cook? Well, throughout the Batch Lady journey, I've always loved recipes that require no cooking in advance, such as burgers that can be frozen raw until needed. These recipes are always tasty, fast and simple to make. I call these Grab and Cook recipes, as they can just be grabbed out of the fridge or freezer and cooked when needed. I first trialled these on my social media and they were a huge hit, with the videos getting millions of views! So I decided to dedicate a whole book to this concept.

Every recipe in this book can be made in advance, with no cooking involved until the night you want to eat it. You'll have minimal washing up, minimal thought needs to go into it, and yet you get maximum results night after night.

I'll give you options so that each meal is personalised to you, and you can decide what suits your needs. You can choose to make a meal to eat straight away, or make it for the freezer for another day, simply by following the colour-coded sections. You can also decide on your method of cooking, with each recipe giving instructions for two or three different cooking methods – whether you prefer an air fryer, an oven, a slow cooker or a pressure cooker, the choice is yours.

Being organised in advance will save you money, time and stress. Imagine coming home to a meal that is already prepared and all you have to do is grab it from the fridge and cook it in your appliance of choice. I hope you love these recipes and that you get started on your Grab and Cook meals right away, so that you instantly know you've got mealtimes covered!

Lots of love,

Suzanne x

GRAB AND COOK EXPLAINED

If you want to make mealtimes easier, my Grab and Cook recipes are for you. These simple recipes have minimal cooking involved and are quick and easy to make and store for whenever they're needed, saving you time, money and headspace.

Grab and Cook does exactly what it says on the tin – it's your own personalised ready meal, just waiting to be grabbed and cooked. All the raw ingredients for the recipe have been put together, then refrigerated or frozen, ready for you to grab and cook whenever you like.

Still getting your head around what they are? Well, just think of all the ready meals you find in the refrigerated section of the supermarket. Little foil or plastic trays, normally containing one or two ready-prepared portions of a meal. Maybe two chicken breasts stuffed and wrapped in bacon, or gammon steaks with a ring of pineapple on top, and a sachet of sauce on the side. Their selling point is convenience – they're a great time-saver. You don't need to think about buying different ingredients and they're portion-controlled, so you know exactly how many to buy. But that convenience comes at a significant price, reflected on your shopping receipt.

My Grab and Cook recipes offer those same benefits but at a fraction of the cost. All the recipes are personalised to your needs, and all can be made in 5–15 minutes. My recipes use convenient short-cuts (see page 10), but you get to decide the exact produce that goes into them; factory-produced ready meals can often involve multiple processes and ingredients not used by home cooks.

Different types of Grab and Cook meals

There are three main types of Grab and Cook recipes, depending on what you are making and how you are cooking them:

- **ONE-POT RECIPES**
  These are often described online as dump bag recipes, meaning that you dump all the ingredients into a freezer bag and freeze them flat. When you want to take it out, you simply grab it and dump it into your slow cooker, pressure cooker or pot. I have many recipes that are prepared in this way, usually soups, stews, casseroles, curries, etc. The benefit is that when you're busy you don't have to think about finding all the different ingredients and getting the recipe ready – instead you just grab the bag from the freezer, follow the instructions that you've written on the bag and cook!

- **ONE-TRAY RECIPES**
  These are recipes that are cooked on a tray, such as fish parcels, chicken goujons or stuffed chicken breasts. These are packaged flat in freezer bags, so you can take out as many as you need, put them on a tray and cook them when you want them. Many baking recipes, such as pastry swirls, tarts and apple turnovers, also come into this category.

- **NO-COOK RECIPES**
  These are desserts, breakfasts, dips and sauces that can be made up in advance but do not need to be cooked when taken out of the freezer, such as cheesecakes, ice cream, traybakes, sorbets, smoothie bowls and hummus.

Grab and Cook meals . . .

1 are your own personalised ready meals, saving you money compared to buying pre-prepared supermarket meals.

2 are quick to make, as there is no initial cooking.

3 are perfect for easy family dinners, as you can just grab them on a busy night.

4 hugely reduce overall time spent in the kitchen compared to making meals from scratch every night.

5 save waste, as all meals are portion-controlled.

6 save money, because you can make them in bulk, with no wasted ingredients.

7 are only cooked once, saving you money on energy bills.

8 can be custom-made for your family or for a fussy eater.

9 allow you to prep meals up to 3 months in advance, so you can be totally organised.

10 are all one-pot or one-pan meals, so there's very little washing up on the night you use them.

11 are very easy to double up, so you can make one for now and one for another night.

THE BATCH LADY LARDER

I'm all about saving time, while still producing good homemade meals! I've always been a fan of a few cheat's products to reduce the time spent in the kitchen. Making my own pastry or roasting peppers from scratch just doesn't work in my busy life and, quite frankly, even if I did have the time, I'd rather be doing something that's more fun.

So throughout these recipes you will see that I have used some of these short-cuts to speed things up. If you prefer to prepare everything from scratch, by all means do, just remember that it will take you longer to make the recipe.

Below I have listed some of the cheat's ingredients used throughout the book and where to find them in the shops.

Cheat's list ✓

- **LEMON CURD**
  beside tinned or baking aisle

- **ELDERFLOWER CORDIAL**
  juice aisle

- **GARLIC NAAN**
  bread section or world food aisle

- **TINNED CARAMEL**
  baking section

- **CARAMELISED ONION CHUTNEY**
  condiment aisle

- **ROASTED RED PEPPERS**
  condiment aisle

- **PIZZA SAUCE**
  condiment or pasta aisle

- **PUFF PASTRY**
  refrigerator section, near butter

- **PIZZA DOUGH**
  refrigerator section, near butter

- **BOMBAY MIX**
  world food aisle or crisp section

- **SMOKED SAUSAGE**
  (*horseshoe-shaped pre-cooked sausage*)
  refrigerator aisle, near cooked meats

- **STRAIGHT-TO-WOK NOODLES**
  pasta and rice aisle

- **PRE-MADE MASH**
  refrigerator section, near ready meals, or in prepared vegetable aisle

- **SPRING ROLL WRAPPERS**
  world food aisle or Asian supermarket

- **READY-MADE CUSTARD**
  storecupboard dessert aisle, near jelly and tinned fruit

Frozen products

I've always been a fan of using products from the freezer, such as frozen veg, fruits and herbs. These save you time, as often they are chopped for you, they save money, as frozen products are cheaper than fresh, and they save waste, as you can simply take out exactly what is needed and store the rest for later. It's a win win! Therefore, I will always give you the quantities needed as a frozen option; however, if you wish to use fresh or dried products, you can simply use the charts below to convert from frozen to fresh or dried.

Vegetables and Fruits

INGREDIENT	FROZEN	FRESH
Chopped/diced onions	1 cup	1 onion, finely chopped
Chopped/diced red onions	1 cup	1 red onion, finely chopped
Mixed sliced peppers	1 cup	1 pepper, deseeded and sliced
Chopped spinach	2 cubes	60g spinach
Sweet potato chunks	1 cup	1 medium sweet potato, peeled and chopped
Butternut squash chunks	1 cup	200g, approx. ⅔ of a whole butternut squash, peeled, deseeded and chopped
Sliced leeks	1 cup	1 small leek, diced
Raspberries	1 cup	125g raspberries
Blueberries	1 cup	110g blueberries
Chopped mango	1 cup	1 mango, peeled, stoned and diced
Chopped pineapple	1 cup	200g, approx. ⅔ of a whole pineapple, peeled, cored and chopped

Herbs and Spices

INGREDIENT	FROZEN	FRESH	DRIED	PURÉED
Coriander	1 teaspoon	1 teaspoon, chopped	⅓ teaspoon	½ teaspoon
Parsley	1 teaspoon	1 teaspoon, chopped	⅓ teaspoon	½ teaspoon
Chilli	1 teaspoon	½ chilli, deseeded and chopped	⅓ teaspoon	½ teaspoon
Basil	1 teaspoon	1 teaspoon, chopped	⅓ teaspoon	½ teaspoon
Rosemary	1 teaspoon	1 teaspoon, chopped	⅓ teaspoon	½ teaspoon
Chopped ginger	1 teaspoon	2.5cm piece, peeled and grated	⅓ teaspoon	½ teaspoon
Thyme	1 teaspoon	1 teaspoon, chopped	⅓ teaspoon	½ teaspoon
Chopped garlic	1 teaspoon	1 clove, crushed	½ teaspoon	½ teaspoon

TOOLKIT

You will have most of the equipment you need in your kitchen already, as the recipes are so simple, however, I would recommend a few basic purchases to help you on your way. These are low-cost and readily available online or in supermarkets.

FREEZER BAGS

Freezer bags are the best way to freeze food. They are great space-savers, as you can freeze everything flat, thus enabling you to get more into your freezer. They are also great for keeping the air out of food, which prevents freezer burn, so your meal should keep longer in the freezer. Freezer bags come in many different sizes according to the brand of bag. I would recommend using a 2.5 litre bag for the majority of recipes that feed four, and a 1.2 litre bag for meals for two. Having a few different-sized freezer bags to hand is always a good idea, especially for recipes that include a small bag of sauce inside a larger bag. Most brands are now washable and reusable, and some are even compostable, so you can minimise your consumption of single-use plastics.

BAGGIE HOLDERS

These are stands that keep your bag open and allow you to have two free hands to prep everything. They are not essential but certainly make the job easier, especially if you are working alone.

CHALK MARKER PENS OR FREEZER LABELS

Chalk marker pens work very well for labelling reusable bags or tubs. You can write directly on the bag, with information such as the name of the recipe, the date it was prepped, the serving size and the cooking info. Leave it to dry for 5 minutes before filling the bag and putting it into your freezer. These markers easily wash off, ready for you to label a new meal when needed.

MEASURING CUPS AND SPOONS

Using cups to measure food is a huge timesaver and saves you getting the scales out and using extra bowls for weighing and measuring. I give both cup measurements and gram measurements in my recipes, so you can choose how you want to work. It's important

to remember that 1 cup is a standard measurement and is not a mug from the shelf – if you want to measure using cups, buy a large set of measuring spoons in cup sizes. These are available from my website.

When measuring in cups, run a knife over the top of the cup so you have a perfectly flat amount. If the recipe says 'scant cup', make the contents slightly less than if you had run a knife over it. This is only important for baking – other meals do not require as much precision.

Cup sizes often differ slightly between countries; below shows the cup sizes used in this book.

1 cup	240ml	16 tablespoons
³⁄₄ cup	180ml	12 tablespoons
²⁄₃ cup	160ml	11 tablespoons
¹⁄₂ cup	120ml	8 tablespoons
¹⁄₃ cup	80ml	5½ tablespoons
¹⁄₄ cup	60ml	4 tablespoons

BAKING TRAYS

Many of the recipes in this book are cooked on a baking tray, and I often suggest flash freezing on a baking tray that fits into a freezer drawer, so a few different sizes of non-stick baking trays will be of benefit.

KITCHEN ALUMINIUM FOIL

Tin foil is great for protecting food in the oven from heat and in the freezer from freezer burn. With foil, my top tip is to use normal household foil that is thin and pliable, and only use one layer. Using multiple layers or thick catering foil can affect the cooking time.

INDIVIDUAL FOIL SHEETS

I usually buy a box of individual pre-cut single foil sheets of 27 x 30cm, which is great for making many of the individual parcel recipes in this book. The thin sheets allow you to create individual portions that can then be bagged up, so you can simply grab as many portions as you need and transfer them to a baking tray in the oven or to the air fryer.

SLOW COOKER, PRESSURE COOKER OR AIR FRYER

This book offers various ways to cook your recipe. Oven times are always given, but if you are looking to save energy costs, a slow cooker, pressure cooker or air fryer will help. There is no need to have them, but they do help with energy costs.

HOW TO USE THIS BOOK

This is the most important page to read, so that you know exactly how the recipes work!

1 CHOOSE TO MAKE AHEAD OR EAT NOW

The recipes in this book use a colour-coded block system. You have the choice whether to make it ahead for the freezer (follow the blue instructions) or to make it to eat now (follow the red instructions).

It's rather like a choose-your-own adventure story, where you decide the ending. So whether you want to make it for the freezer or cook it fresh, I have you covered!

 BLUE = IF MAKING AHEAD TO FREEZE

Follow these instructions if you want to make the recipes for the freezer ahead of time. The cooking instructions will also be in blue – these are either cooking instructions from frozen or information on how to defrost before cooking.

If you are making for now, skip the blue block and start on the red . . .

 RED = IF COOKING NOW

Follow these instructions to make the recipes to eat right away. The method will tell you exactly how to make it, and the cooking instructions are based on the recipe being cooked from fresh.

Occasionally, if a recipe has a similar method, you will be asked to jump between the sections. Simply follow the step-by-step instructions and you can't go wrong.

2 CHOOSE YOUR PREFERRED WAY TO COOK YOUR MEALS

Nowadays, we have so many different cooking appliance options, and we all have our favourites. Some may choose the traditional oven with stovetop, whereas others would rather use a slow cooker or pressure cooker, or indeed the newest kid on the block, the air fryer. So for this book I really wanted to leave the choice of cooking up to you as much as possible. See page 16 for more information on which appliance to use.

If you'd like to choose your recipes based on using your favourite appliance, see pages 26–29 for a list of all the recipes in the book sorted by appliance.

Vegetarian and Vegan Options

50 of the recipes in this book are vegetarian (identified with 'V' in a circle by the recipe title), and 16 are vegan (identified with 'VE'). Nowadays, many households need to cater for different food preferences, so I wanted to allow for that. I'm a fan of making the same meal for everyone, with a few tweaks to accommodate dietary requirements, so I have included tips on recipes that you can make vegetarian and vegan just by substituting ingredients. This means you can serve everyone a similar meal, but some portions can be vegetarian or vegan, keeping everyone happy and keeping costs to a minimum.

CHILLI CHEESE & CHUTNEY NAAN TOASTIES

I love these Indian-inspired naan toasties – they make the perfect weekend breakfast or brunch.

Prep: 5–10 minutes | **Makes:** 4

1 cup (140g) grated Cheddar

1 cup (140g) grated mozzarella

4 spring onions, finely diced

a knob of fresh ginger, grated

1 green chilli, seeds removed and finely diced

a large handful of fresh coriander, roughly chopped

4 mini garlic naan breads

4 tsp mango chutney

 IF MAKING AHEAD TO FREEZE

1 Mix together the grated cheeses, spring onions, ginger, green chilli and coriander in a bowl.
2 Gently slice all the naan breads open with a sharp knife. Spread a teaspoon of mango chutney on each of the bottom halves, then divide the cheese mix between all 4 naans and pop the lids on to enclose the filling. Wrap each one individually in tin foil.
3 Put the wrapped toasties into a large labelled freezer bag and freeze.

OVEN

Preheat the oven to 200°C. Place the frozen toasties, still wrapped in their foil, on a baking tray. Put them into the oven for 15 minutes, then open them up and cook for a further 6 minutes to crisp up.

AIR FRYER

Preheat the air fryer to 180°C. Place the frozen toasties, still wrapped in their foil, into the air fryer and cook for 12 minutes, then open them up and cook for a further 2 minutes to crisp up.

 IF COOKING NOW

Follow the method in the 'making ahead to freeze' section up until the end of step 2.

OVEN

Preheat the oven to 200°C. Place the wrapped toasties on a baking tray and put them into the oven for 10 minutes, then open up the top of the foil and cook for a further 5 minutes.

AIR FRYER

Preheat the air fryer to 180°C. Place the wrapped toasties into the air fryer and cook for 5 minutes, then open up the top of the foil and cook for a further 5 minutes.

TIP
Add a fried egg to each toastie with a scattering of extra spring onions for a delicious brunch.

44

HOW TO CHOOSE YOUR COOKING METHOD

Let's talk cooking methods! Each of us will have a preferred option depending on what appliances we have. Here are my top tips on the appliances I use so that you can make an informed decision. If you are thinking of purchasing any of these, I have included advice on the sizes or styles I recommend.

 ## Slow cooker

I adore slow cookers – they are so easy to use and are low-cost to buy and run. You can simply empty the meal from the freezer bag into the slow cooker in the morning, get it going, and when you come in from work a lovely meal awaits you. Slow cookers are great for soups, stews, chillis, casseroles, etc., and I tend to use mine more in the winter.

SLOW COOKERS COME IN DIFFERENT SIZES:

1.2–2.3 litre slow cooker	4–4.5 litre slow cooker	5.5–7 litre slow cooker
=	=	=
great for two people	will feed four people	ideal for four to six people

Slow cooking is great for saving money on energy, as it stops you having your oven on low for hours, but it also has another great cost saving in that you can use cheaper cuts of meat, and because they are cooked low and slow, they will soften to become perfectly tender. Top tip: remember you should not lift the lid during the cooking process (unless specifically stated in the recipe), as the steam created inside is needed to keep the slow cooker at the correct temperature. The more you open the lid, the more heat you let out.

HIGH AND LOW SETTINGS

With all slow cookers you can choose to cook on high or low. The high setting usually cooks in half the time of the low setting. If you are new to cooking with a slow cooker, it can be difficult to know what setting to choose.

TIPS

· *If you are out for the full day, cooking on the low setting would be the best option.*

· *If you have used cheaper cuts of meat, cooking on the low setting for a longer period of time is best.*

· *If you are making a meal at lunchtime and want to eat it for dinner, choose the high setting.*

BROWNING MEAT

Browning meat before putting it into a slow cooker isn't strictly necessary – you can just dump it all in together. However, it is well worth the effort, as it adds a rich flavour, texture and colour to your finished dish. In many of the recipes in this book, you are asked to freeze the meat separately: this is so you can brown it before adding the rest of the ingredients. If you don't want to brown the meat, you can simply put everything in together.

If your slow cooker does not have a sauté function for browning meat, fear not, you can brown it in a pan before putting it into the slow cooker.

Pressure cooker

Pressure cookers work like slow cookers but cook food much faster. The sealed lid keeps all the steam in, creating a pressured environment so that everything cooks much quicker, reducing the amount of energy that you use. Pressure cookers use on average half the amount of energy of normal stovetop cooking. They are great if you struggle to be organised enough to put things into the slow cooker in the morning before work. A pressure cooker does the same work but in a lot less time, so you can pop it on after work and it will be done in no time at all.

It's great for dense veggies such as root veg, as well as pulses, and brilliant for cheaper cuts of meat that would usually take quite a long time to cook on the hob. They will take no time at all in a pressure cooker. You do need to use the exact amount of liquid stated for the recipe to work correctly, so be sure to stick to the exact quantity of water or stock given.

Please be aware that there are numerous different pressure cookers, from stovetop to multi-functioning electric ones, all with different functions. All the recipes in this book were tested and created using a basic 5 litre Instant Pot pressure cooker, so you may need to adjust cooking times slightly if you are using a different one.

Air fryer

As we all try to use less energy and reduce our bills, many of us have turned to air fryers as a convenient way to cook food, and I have to say I love mine. I have included lots of recipes suitable for the air fryer in this book, and many of them can be cooked straight from frozen, making life very simple indeed.

The recipes in this book are for a family of four, so if you have a small two-person air fryer, you may have to cook some of the recipes in two batches. I used a double-drawer air fryer for testing, so I could cook the recipe all at once by dividing it between the drawers.

If you're single or a couple, the air fryer is particularly suitable. Many of my recipes in Light Bites & Lunches are great to cook in the morning and take to work – using the air fryer for these means it only takes a few minutes in the morning to get lunch ready, so it's great for these smaller meals. If you are looking to purchase an air fryer and you are feeding a family, I would suggest buying a large 9–11 litre appliance.

Oven

I don't think I need to say much about this – we all have an oven and we know how to use it, although we may be trying to use it less these days, due to rising energy costs. If you only have an oven to cook with, consider cooking two meals at a time, then you can eat one that night and reheat the other in the microwave the following day. This uses less energy than cooking in the oven every night. I have included oven times in nearly all the recipes, and all are based on conventional oven temperatures. If you're using a fan-assisted oven, reduce the temperature by 20°C.

TIP

When you make a recipe to keep in the freezer, my top tip is to add the cooking instructions to the bag; that way you don't need to find the exact page in this book to work out how to cook it. For example: 'Cook from frozen in the air fryer for 15 mins at 180°C.' This will make your life much easier on busy nights!

OK, Let's get cooking!

LET'S BATCH!

Now that you know what these recipes are about and how to make them, let's talk about how to batch them. So what is batching? Batching is grouping tasks together to do them all at once. It's a perfect productivity tool to help you get things done quickly and efficiently. No one wants to be cooking from scratch and cleaning multiple dishes night after night. Batching your meals allows you to make a few at a time, so you always have one ready to go no matter how busy your day has been.

It's very quick and easy to get started with batching, especially with these Grab and Cook recipes, as no actual cooking is involved when you are making them for the freezer. With each recipe only taking on average 5–10 minutes, you can make three or four meals in as little as 30 minutes! Below are some of my top tips and helpful advice to get you started.

Choosing your quantity

The recipes in this book are all based on cooking for a family of four. But remember, you are making your own meals so you can change them to suit your family.

ONLY TWO OF YOU?

If you are a couple, I would still suggest making the whole recipe for four and simply packaging it as two meals. This way you automatically make double portions without having to think about it.

ARE YOU FLYING SOLO?

Consider halving the recipe – this gives you two portions, so again you will have an extra portion for whenever it's needed. The only recipes you cannot halve are the ones made for the slow cooker or pressure cooker, as these need a specific amount of liquid in them to work, so halving the recipe will cause problems. Instead, why not see if you can team up with a friend? They could make one full recipe and you could make a different one, then you could swap half of each so you get a good variety of meals with minimal effort.

BATCH WITH FRIENDS

If you're cooking for one or two, consider getting a few friends together for a batching evening. These can be great fun – each person arrives with the ingredients for a single recipe and you make it at the table as you sit, chat, gossip and drink a cheeky glass of something. At the end of the night, simply divide the recipe portions between you so you all go home with a selection of meals. On a cost per pound basis, it's much cheaper to buy a pack of four chicken breasts than it is to buy a single one, so you will find that buying as a group helps. The oven and air fryer one-tray meals are especially good for splitting.

GOING LARGE

Are you a family of five or six? Most of the meals will be easy to scale up. If you are making recipes that have individual portions, such as the fish parcels or the chicken breasts, these are particularly easy to add another few portions to. If you are making the slow cooker/pressure cooker meals, I would suggest keeping the recipe as it is, but serving more sides with it, such as garlic bread, extra potatoes, extra salad, etc.

MAKING DOUBLE

Once you have tried a recipe and like it, I suggest making double, so instead of making one meal for four people, you can double the ingredients and make two meals for four people. If you are going to the trouble of finding all the ingredients and laying them out for one recipe, you may as well simply double the ingredients and make an extra meal for another night. Doubling a recipe takes on average only 3 minutes longer, yet it gives you a whole extra night off. It's the perfect way to start batching if you're a beginner, and a great way to build up a stock of extra meals in your freezer. If you're having one for tonight and one for the freezer, it's very easy to keep your portions separate – just add one to a cooking pot, and the other directly into a freezer bag.

PORTION CONTROL

Portioning meals properly is a great way to stay healthy, save money and save food waste. A lot of the recipes in this book are already portioned out for you into individual servings or parcels. However, if you have doubled up, say, a curry or a stew, it can be hard sometimes to work out how to portion it. The best way is to use the measuring cups that I recommend in the toolkit section (see page 12). The general rule is that one level cup of scoopable food (bolognese/curry/stew, etc.) will feed an adult, whereas half a cup should be enough to feed a child under 10.

Batch a variety of meals

MAKE A LIST OF MEALS YOU WANT TO MAKE

Batching is often thought of as making a huge vat of the same type of meal and eating it constantly until it's finished, but this is far from the truth. Variety, after all, is the spice of life! When deciding what to batch, it's good to choose different types of meals to put into your freezer so you constantly have a good range to choose from. Why not put aside a few minutes to grab a cuppa and make a list of all the meals you would like to make from the book, ensuring you have a good variety.

SPEED BATCHING YOUR VARIETY OF MEALS

If you are looking to make your meals superfast, choose those that have similar ingredients. For example, say you are going to make the fish parcels on page 96. There are four different versions of fish parcels in the book; making a few different ones at the same time will get you in the swing of parcel-making and you will automatically make them more quickly than if you were swapping between, say, a soup recipe and fish parcels.

MONEY SAVING

Batching will save you money. Buying larger packs of food is cheaper per kg than buying smaller packs, so doubling a recipe will instantly reduce the price per recipe and portion. With some of the recipes in this book, I give guidance as to other recipes that match up with the one you are making – for instance, in the Easy Bakes chapter, a few of the recipes require a small amount of condensed milk, so rather than waste the rest of the tin, why not prepare other recipes with condensed milk at the same time?

FREEZING AND DEFROSTING

New appliances are constantly marketed as the answer to our problems, something that will revolutionise our lives, and we do love to try new things. The humble freezer hums away in the background, with little thought given to it, but it is perhaps the greatest time-saving appliance of all!

If you want a hassle-free life when it comes to cooking, your freezer is your friend, your secret weapon, your single most important kitchen tool. By using your freezer you're able to cook delicious meals, save food waste, save time, save money and most importantly save headspace. With Grab and Cook bags, in one hour you can have a week's worth of meals in your freezer.

Freezing

HOW TO FREEZE MEALS
Use the guidelines below to get to grips with the simplest and safest way of preparing meals for your freezer.

- *When making a recipe that contains ready-frozen vegetables, work fast and get them back into the freezer as soon as possible to avoid them starting to defrost.*

- *Keep the outside of the freezer bag dry at all times – this will prevent it sticking to other bags in the freezer.*

- *Clearly label your bags with the name of the meal, the date it was made, the serving size and the cooking instructions. If the recipe states, for example, 'to cook, add ½ cup of water and a tub of crème fraîche', write this instruction on the bag. The more information you write, the easier it will be to cook.*

- *Label your bag before filling it, as it's much easier to write on when it's flat and empty, and it gives the ink time to dry.*

- *Where possible, freeze meals flat, expelling any excess air before sealing. Laying the meals*

flat means you can stack them on top of each other, making the most efficient use of space in your freezer.

- *If you are freezing multiple meals at a time, space them out around your freezer until they're frozen, then stack them on top of each other. This method will help meals freeze faster and stop them freezing or sticking together.*

FLASH FREEZING
In some of my recipes, you will see the instruction to flash freeze the food on a tray for a certain amount of time before packing it into freezer bags. Flash freezing is a process that allows you to freeze food without it sticking together or losing its shape, so you end up with individual portions that you can grab out of the bag, rather than having to defrost the whole bag. Simply find a small tray that fits into one of your freezer drawers, line the tray with baking parchment, then put whatever needs to be frozen on the tray in individual portions, making sure they have space around them. Once frozen, these can go into a labelled freezer bag and be stored flat and airtight in the freezer. See page 25 for an image of this process.

DIVIDED FREEZING METHOD
If you want to cook from frozen, one of the main challenges is how to get a large frozen-bag-size square of, for example, soup or stew into a round pot

or a slow cooker! It's actually very easy: before you freeze your bag of food, lay it flat on a tray and mark deep lines with a ruler or skewer down the middle and across the bag, so that the bag looks like the large portion inside has been divided into four. Then carefully freeze. This will allow you to snap off each portion and fit the small frozen portions into a slow cooker or round pot. If you want the meal to cook even quicker, divide it into more sections. The image opposite shows you how to do this.

SMALL FREEZER STORAGE

By storing your Grab and Cook meals flat in bags and stacking them like library books, you can get on average 15 family meals in one freezer drawer. So even if you have the smallest of freezers, you can still be organised with Grab and Cook meals in your freezer.

STORING MEALS IN YOUR FRIDGE ONLY

If you don't have the space to freeze meals ahead, you can still make a few in advance and store them in your fridge. This will help you to still be organised for a few days ahead. Simply prepare two or three meals for the next few nights and store them in the fridge, being sure to mark any sell-by dates on the bags so you know which ones to eat first.

Defrosting

There are three main ways to defrost food: in the fridge, in cold water, or in the microwave – choose what suits your needs best! Defrosting meals that have been frozen flat is fast: they are thin, so unlike freezing in tubs, they will defrost quickly. Once a meal is fully defrosted, you have 24 hours before it has to be cooked.

· **IN YOUR FRIDGE**

If the recipe says to defrost before cooking, you can place the bag in the fridge overnight and it will be defrosted by the next day. Remember to always place it on a tray or in a dish to catch any water that collects as it defrosts.

· **THE COLD WATER METHOD**

Need something defrosted fast? Place your sealed bag, with the seal above the water, in a basin or tub of cold (never hot!) water. Within 20 minutes, the meal should be on its way to defrosting. This is my favourite way to defrost, as it's so quick – it's a great method to use if you have forgotten to take something out of the freezer.

· **IN THE MICROWAVE**

Most microwaves have dedicated defrosting programmes. Always remove the food from the freezer bag and put it into a microwave-safe plate or bowl. Then simply follow the manufacturer's guidelines for your specific model, remembering to stir your food part way through the defrosting cycle.

TIP

Struggling to remember to take things out of the freezer? Simply set an alarm on your phone that goes off at 6pm every night, reminding you to take tomorrow night's meal out of the freezer. It's a time you're generally in the kitchen anyway, so it's an easy chore. Most of the recipes in this book are cooked from frozen, so even if you completely forget, it shouldn't be a concern.

These are my top tips on using your freezer for Grab and Cook recipes. I have given more detailed information on making the most of your freezer on pages 240 and 241, and I really recommend having a read through when you have the time.

Cooking from frozen

Want to make life easier and skip the defrost stage? The recipes below can all be cooked directly from frozen. If you find you have forgotten to take something out the freezer, see if you have any of these recipes, and simply cook from frozen. My top tip is to always keep a few in your freezer, so you always have emergency meals to hand.

RECIPES BY APPLIANCE

Why not choose your recipe based on the appliance you'd like to cook it in?

 ## Air fryer

Oven

Hob

BREAKFAST & BRUNCH

LIGHT BITES & LUNCHES

WEEKNIGHT

FAKEAWAYS

FAMILY & FRIENDS

Slow cooker

LIGHT BITES & LUNCHES

WEEKNIGHT

FAKEAWAYS

FAMILY & FRIENDS

 # Pressure cooker

LIGHT BITES & LUNCHES

WEEKNIGHT

FAKEAWAYS

FAMILY & FRIENDS

 # Microwave

WEEKNIGHT

No cooking needed

BREAKFAST & BRUNCH

LIGHT BITES & LUNCHES

EASY BAKES

DESSERTS

BREAKFAST
& ——
BRUNCH

BLUEBERRY BREAKFAST SCONES

Blueberry scones are one of my favourite things, and they are brilliant for a slow weekend brekkie with a big cup of tea or coffee. Make a double batch and freeze them, so you always have homemade scones for people popping round.

Prep: 10 minutes | **Makes:** 6 large scones

2 cups (220g) self-raising flour

1 tsp baking powder

65g cold butter, cut into cubes

¼ cup (50g) caster sugar

150g fresh blueberries

1 egg

½ cup (120ml) milk, plus 2 tbsp

2 tbsp demerara sugar

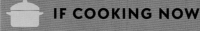

❄ IF MAKING AHEAD TO FREEZE

1 In a large mixing bowl, rub together the flour, baking powder, butter and caster sugar until the mix looks like breadcrumbs. Stir through the fresh blueberries.

2 Combine the egg and ½ cup of milk in a separate jug, then pour into the dry mix and stir gently until it comes together in a rough dough.

3 Tip the dough onto a work surface and bring together into a ball. Roll it out, using a rolling pin, to form a circle 4cm deep.

4 Cut the dough like a cake to give you 6 triangles.

5 Brush each triangle with a little of the extra milk and sprinkle over the demerara sugar.

6 Open your large labelled freezer bag. Keeping the bag flat, put in the scones, leaving space so they don't stick together. If stacking on top of each other, add a layer of baking parchment to stop them sticking. Place flat in the freezer until fully frozen.

▢ OVEN

Preheat the oven to 190°C. Cook the frozen scones on a lined baking tray for 20–25 minutes, until golden.

▢ AIR FRYER

Preheat the air fryer to 190°C. Cook the scones for 10–12 minutes, until golden.

🍲 IF COOKING NOW

Follow the method in the 'making ahead to freeze' section up until the end of step 5.

▢ OVEN

Preheat the oven to 190°C. Cook the scones on a lined baking tray for 18–22 minutes, until golden.

▢ AIR FRYER

Preheat the air fryer to 190°C. Cook the scones for 9–10 minutes, until golden.

TIP

I like to serve these with butter and blueberry jam.

BRIOCHE CINNAMON FRENCH TOAST STICKS

These French toast fingers are so delicious, and are a real treat for breakfast. The brioche bread makes for an extra soft middle and a lovely crisp outside. I recommend buying a loaf of brioche and slicing it yourself to get nice thick slices.

Prep: 10 minutes | **Serves:** 4

6 thick slices of brioche bread

3 eggs

¾ cup (180ml) whole milk

1 tsp vanilla extract

½ tsp ground cinnamon

To cook:
a knob of butter or
a little vegetable oil,
if air-frying

 IF MAKING AHEAD TO FREEZE

1   Cut each slice of brioche into 3 sticks.
2   Put the eggs, milk, vanilla extract and cinnamon into a shallow bowl and whisk lightly with a fork.
3   Dip the brioche sticks into the egg mix, coating them thoroughly one at a time and putting them on a lined tray as you go.
4   Place the tray in the freezer and leave to flash freeze for 1 hour, then remove and put into a labelled freezer bag.

 HOB

Put a knob of butter into a non-stick frying pan and place on a medium heat. Carefully add the frozen brioche sticks in batches and cook for 3–4 minutes on each side, until golden.

 AIR FRYER

Preheat the air fryer to 180°C. Drizzle the frozen brioche sticks with a little oil and place on a sheet of baking parchment in the air fryer. Cook for 10 minutes, flipping them over halfway through, until golden.

 IF COOKING NOW

Follow the method in the 'making ahead to freeze' section up until the end of step 3.

HOB

Put a knob of butter into a non-stick frying pan and place on a medium heat. Carefully add the brioche fingers in batches and cook for 2–3 minutes on each side, until golden.

 AIR FRYER

Preheat the air fryer to 180°C. Drizzle the frozen brioche sticks with a little oil and place on a sheet of baking parchment in the air fryer. Cook for 7 minutes, flipping them over halfway through, until golden.

NUTTY ENERGY BALLS

These are the perfect quick breakfast on the go. They are packed full of slow-release carbs to keep you going until lunchtime, and they also work great as a lunchbox snack or afternoon pick-me-up.

Prep: 5 minutes | **Makes:** 12

1¼ cups (200g) pitted dates

½ cup (50g) fine oats

1 cup (150g) ground almonds

2 tbsp cocoa powder

2 tbsp smooth peanut butter

2 tbsp coconut oil

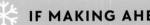 **IF MAKING AHEAD TO FREEZE**

1 Put everything into a food processor and blitz until you have a thick paste.
2 Tip out onto a work surface and roll into 12 evenly sized balls.

3 Place the balls in a labelled freezer bag and freeze flat.

READY TO EAT

Remove from the freezer and leave to defrost – they will take around 1 hour to defrost at room temperature.

 IF MAKING NOW

1 Follow the method in the 'making ahead to freeze' section up until the end of step 2, then put the balls into the fridge for 1 hour to firm up.

2 They are now ready to eat whenever you fancy. They are best kept in a container in the fridge and will keep for up to 5 days.

BAKED MAPLE & ALMOND NECTARINES

These are the ultimate yoghurt topper and a great way to start the day. You could also enjoy these as a dessert with some ice cream.

Prep: 5 minutes | **Serves:** 4

4 ripe nectarines, cut in half and stones removed

2 tbsp maple syrup

½ cup (60g) whole (skin-on) almonds, roughly chopped

1 tsp vanilla extract

 IF MAKING AHEAD TO FREEZE

Put all the ingredients into a large labelled freezer bag and give them a good mix. Place flat in the freezer.

OVEN

Preheat the oven to 180°C. Put the frozen nectarines, skin side down, into an ovenproof dish and cook for 12–14 minutes, until soft. If your nectarines are very ripe, reduce the cooking time by a few minutes.

AIR FRYER

Preheat the air fryer to 180°C. Put the frozen nectarines, skin side down, into an air fryer-safe dish and cook for 8–10 minutes, until soft. If your nectarines are very ripe, reduce the cooking time by a few minutes.

 IF COOKING NOW

Put all the ingredients into a bowl and mix.

OVEN

Preheat the oven to 180°C. Put everything into an ovenproof dish, making sure the nectarine halves are skin side down, and cook for 9–10 minutes, until soft. If your nectarines are very ripe, reduce the cooking time by a few minutes.

AIR FRYER

Preheat the air fryer to 180°C. Put everything into an air fryer-safe dish, making sure the nectarine halves are skin side down, and cook for 6–8 minutes, until soft. If your nectarines are very ripe, reduce the cooking time by a few minutes.

TIP
Serve with granola and Greek yoghurt (or plant-based yoghurt to keep it vegan).

RASPBERRY, WHITE CHOCOLATE & PECAN BRIOCHE BAKE

This decadent brioche bake is so delicious, and the perfect weekend brunch for friends and family! Dust with icing sugar and add a dollop of Greek yoghurt, if you like. Yum!

Prep: 5–10 minutes | **Serves:** 4–6

8 butter brioche rolls (approx. 280g)

1 cup (130g) frozen or fresh raspberries

120g white chocolate, cut into rough chunks

½ cup (50g) pecans, roughly chopped

4 eggs

½ cup (120ml) double cream

1 cup (240ml) whole milk

¼ cup (60ml) maple syrup

1 tsp vanilla extract

❄ IF MAKING AHEAD TO FREEZE

1 Tear the brioche rolls into pieces and put them into a large labelled freezer bag along with the raspberries, the chunks of white chocolate and the chopped pecans.

2 Put the eggs, double cream, milk, maple syrup and vanilla extract into a mixing jug. Whisk together with a fork, then pour into the freezer bag. Give everything a good mix and freeze flat.

OVEN

Remove from the freezer and leave to fully defrost. Preheat the oven to 180°C. Pour everything into a lightly greased, medium-sized ovenproof dish and place in the oven for 30–40 minutes, until golden.

AIR FRYER

Remove from the freezer and leave to fully defrost. Preheat the air fryer to 180°C. Pour the mix into a lightly greased air fryer-safe dish and cook for 10 minutes, then remove and cover well with tin foil. Return to the air fryer for another 10–12 minutes, until golden.

IF COOKING NOW

1 Put the eggs, double cream, milk, maple syrup and vanilla extract into a mixing bowl and whisk with a fork.
2 Tear the brioche rolls into pieces and add to the mixing bowl along with the raspberries, the chunks of white chocolate and the chopped pecans.
3 Mix and leave to sit for 20 minutes.

OVEN

Preheat the oven to 180°C. Pour the mix into a lightly greased ovenproof dish and place in the oven for 30–40 minutes, until golden.

AIR FRYER

Preheat the air fryer to 180°C. Pour the mix into a lightly greased air fryer-safe dish and cook for 10 minutes, then remove and cover well with tin foil. Return to the air fryer for another 10–12 minutes, until golden.

TROPICAL SMOOTHIE BOWL

Fresh, fruity and thick, this smoothie bowl will transport you to a tropical beach!
Top with whatever you fancy – I like to add some toasted coconut flakes and granola.

Prep: 5 minutes　　|　　**Makes:** 2 big bowls or 4 smaller bowls

1 cup (140g) frozen chopped mango, or 1 fresh mango, peeled, stoned and chopped into chunks

2 bananas, peeled and sliced

1 cup (150g) frozen or fresh strawberries

2 passion fruits, halved and seeds scooped out

½ cup (110g) coconut yoghurt

To make:
1 cup (240ml) cold water

❄ IF MAKING AHEAD TO FREEZE

Put everything into a large labelled freezer bag or individual serving size freezer bags, mix and freeze flat.

READY TO MAKE

Remove from the freezer, put into a food processor or blender along with the water, and blitz until smooth. Pour into bowls and top with whatever you fancy.

🍲 IF MAKING NOW

Put everything into a food processor or blender along with the water and blitz until smooth. Pour into bowls and top with whatever you fancy.

CHILLI CHEESE & CHUTNEY NAAN TOASTIES

I love these Indian-inspired naan toasties – they make the perfect weekend breakfast or brunch.

Prep: 5–10 minutes | **Makes:** 4

1 cup (140g) grated Cheddar

1 cup (140g) grated mozzarella

4 spring onions, finely diced

a knob of fresh ginger, grated

1 green chilli, seeds removed and finely diced

a large handful of fresh coriander, roughly chopped

4 mini garlic naan breads

4 tsp mango chutney

 IF MAKING AHEAD TO FREEZE

1   Mix together the grated cheeses, spring onions, ginger, green chilli and coriander in a bowl.
2   Gently slice all the naan breads open with a sharp knife. Spread a teaspoon of mango chutney on each of the bottom halves, then divide the cheese mix between all 4 naans and pop the lids on to enclose the filling. Wrap each one individually in tin foil.
3   Put the wrapped toasties into a large labelled freezer bag and freeze.

OVEN

Preheat the oven to 200°C. Place the frozen toasties, still wrapped in their foil, on a baking tray. Put them into the oven for 15 minutes, then open them up and cook for a further 6 minutes to crisp up.

AIR FRYER

Preheat the air fryer to 180°C. Place the frozen toasties, still wrapped in their foil, into the air fryer and cook for 12 minutes, then open them up and cook for a further 2 minutes to crisp up.

 IF COOKING NOW

Follow the method in the 'making ahead to freeze' section up until the end of step 2.

OVEN

Preheat the oven to 200°C. Place the wrapped toasties on a baking tray and put them into the oven for 10 minutes, then open up the top of the foil and cook for a further 5 minutes.

AIR FRYER

Preheat the air fryer to 180°C. Place the wrapped toasties into the air fryer and cook for 5 minutes, then open up the top of the foil and cook for a further 5 minutes.

TIP

Add a fried egg to each toastie with a scattering of extra spring onions for a delicious brunch.

GREENS SMOOTHIE BOWL

These smoothie bowls are packed full of the good stuff! They are so easy to make, and they're great to have in the freezer to grab for a quick breakfast. You can have a lot of fun adding different toppings – try a combination of granola with various seeds, nuts and fruits!

Prep: 5 minutes | **Makes:** 2 big bowls or 4 smaller bowls

2 bananas, peeled and cut into chunks

80g fresh spinach or 2 cubes of frozen chopped spinach

2 kiwi fruits, peeled and cut into chunks

1 cup (140g) frozen chopped mango, or 1 fresh mango, peeled, stoned and chopped into chunks

½ cup (110g) Greek yoghurt

2 tbsp almond or peanut butter

To make:
1 cup (240ml) cold water

 IF MAKING AHEAD TO FREEZE

Put everything into a large labelled freezer bag or individual serving size freezer bags, mix and freeze flat.

READY TO MAKE

Remove from the freezer, put into a food processor or blender along with the water, and blitz until smooth. Pour into bowls and top with whatever you fancy.

 IF MAKING NOW

Put everything into a food processor or blender along with the water and blitz until smooth. Pour into bowls and top with whatever you fancy.

TIP
To make this smoothie bowl vegan, use a plant-based yoghurt.

HAM & CHEESE CROISSANT BAKE

This croissant bake is the perfect weekend treat. Oozy cheese and chopped ham nestled between flaky croissants! Great to share with friends and family.

Prep: 5 minutes | **Serves:** 4–6

6 medium all-butter croissants

¾ cup (105g) grated cheese (any cheese)

6 large slices of ham, diced

2 tsp Dijon mustard (optional)

4 eggs

½ cup (120ml) milk

½ cup (120ml) double cream

salt and pepper

 ## IF MAKING AHEAD TO FREEZE

1 Tear the croissants roughly into pieces and put them into a large labelled freezer bag with the grated cheese and diced ham.
2 Put the optional Dijon mustard, the eggs, milk, cream and a good grind of salt and pepper into a mixing jug and whisk together with a fork.
3 Pour the liquid into the freezer bag, mix gently to combine with the croissants, then seal and freeze flat.

 ### OVEN

Remove from the freezer and leave to fully defrost. Preheat the oven to 180°C. Pour everything into a greased ovenproof dish and place in the oven for 30–40 minutes, until golden.

 ### AIR FRYER

Remove from the freezer and leave to fully defrost. Preheat the air fryer to 180°C. Pour the mix into a greased air fryer-safe dish and cook for 10 minutes, then remove and cover well with tin foil. Place back into the air fryer and cook for a further 10–12 minutes, until golden.

 ## IF COOKING NOW

1 Put the optional Dijon mustard, the eggs, milk, cream and a good grind of salt and pepper into a mixing bowl and whisk with a fork.
2 Tear the croissants roughly into pieces and add to the mixing bowl along with the grated cheese and diced ham.
3 Mix together gently and leave to sit for 20 minutes.

OVEN

Preheat the oven to 180°C. Pour the mix into a greased ovenproof dish and place in the oven for 30–40 minutes, until golden.

AIR FRYER

Preheat the air fryer to 180°C. Pour the mix into a greased air fryer-safe dish and cook for 10 minutes, then remove and cover well with tin foil. Place back into the air fryer and cook for a further 10–12 minutes, until golden.

TIP
To make this vegetarian, use plant-based ham or sliced mushrooms instead of ham.

CINNAMON-SPICED PLUMS

These delicious spiced plums are perfect on top of your morning bowl of porridge. They are so simple to make – why not make a big batch and get them into the freezer!

Prep: 5 minutes | **Serves:** 4

6 large ripe plums, cut in half and stones removed

1 tsp ground cinnamon

2 tbsp runny honey

juice of 1 orange

1 tsp vanilla extract

 IF MAKING AHEAD TO FREEZE

Put all the ingredients into a large labelled freezer bag and give everything a good shake to mix together. Seal the bag and freeze flat.

 OVEN

Preheat the oven to 180°C. Put the frozen plums, skin side down, into an ovenproof dish and cook for 10–12 minutes, until soft. If the plums are very ripe, they will take slightly less time to cook.

 AIR FRYER

Preheat the air fryer to 180°C. Put the frozen plums, skin side down, into an air fryer-safe dish and cook for 8–9 minutes, until soft. If the plums are very ripe, they will take slightly less time to cook.

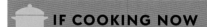 **IF COOKING NOW**

Put all the ingredients into a large bowl and mix well.

OVEN

Preheat the oven to 180°C. Put the plums, skin side down, into an ovenproof dish and cook for 9–10 minutes, until soft. If the plums are very ripe, they will take slightly less time to cook.

 AIR FRYER

Preheat the air fryer to 180°C. Put the plums, skin side down, into an air fryer-safe dish and cook for 7–8 minutes, until soft. If the plums are very ripe, they will take slightly less time to cook.

APPLE & BLUEBERRY OVERNIGHT OATS

This is a great make-ahead breakfast. It's not freezable, but you can make the oats up at the start of the week and they will keep for up to 3 days in the fridge. I like to use old jam jars to store individual portions, but any Tupperware will do.

Prep: 5 minutes | **Serves:** 4

1½ cups plus 1 tbsp (160g) jumbo oats

1½ cups (360ml) milk (or any other milk alternative)

4 heaped tbsp Greek yoghurt

2 eating apples, peeled, cored and grated

4 handfuls of frozen or fresh blueberries

4 tsp runny honey

ground cinnamon, to sprinkle

 IF MAKING AHEAD TO FREEZE

1 Find four small containers with lids. Divide the oats, milk and Greek yoghurt between each one, and mix well to combine.
2 Distribute the grated apple between the 4 containers, add a handful of blueberries to each one, drizzle a teaspoon of honey over each one, add a sprinkle of cinnamon and mix again. Pop the lids on the containers and keep in the fridge for whenever they're needed.

READY TO EAT

Remove from the fridge and enjoy.

TIP

To make this vegan, use plant-based milk and yoghurt, and substitute the honey with a vegan sweetener.

LIGHT BITES
&
LUNCHES

HERBY CHEESE & PROSCIUTTO PINWHEELS

These are so addictive, and they're a great easy lunch option, made with pizza dough to keep you powering on through your day. Great to throw into the air fryer in the morning, ready to take to work for lunch on the go!

Prep: 5–10 minutes | **Makes:** 8

1 roll of ready-made pizza dough (400g)

6 slices of prosciutto

150g Boursin cheese

10 sun-dried tomatoes in oil, drained and finely diced

a handful of fresh basil leaves

 IF MAKING AHEAD TO FREEZE

1 Unroll the pizza dough, keeping it on its paper.
2 Layer the prosciutto on top so it covers all the dough.
3 Crumble over the Boursin, then scatter over the sun-dried tomatoes and the basil leaves.

4 Roll up the dough, starting from a short end, until you have one big roll. Cut into 8 slices, using a sharp knife.
5 Open your large labelled freezer bag. Keeping the bag flat, put in the pinwheels, leaving space so they don't stick together. Place flat in the freezer until fully frozen.

 OVEN

Preheat the oven to 190°C. Place the frozen pinwheels on a lined baking tray and cook for 20–23 minutes, until golden.

 AIR FRYER

Preheat the air fryer to 190°C. Put in the frozen pinwheels and cook them for 16 minutes, flipping them over halfway through, until golden.

 IF COOKING NOW

Follow the method in the 'making ahead to freeze' section up until the end of step 4.

OVEN

Preheat the oven to 190°C. Place the pinwheels on a lined baking tray and cook for 18 minutes, until golden.

AIR FRYER

Preheat the air fryer to 190°C. Put in the pinwheels and cook them for 14 minutes, flipping them over halfway through, until golden.

TIP

Great on their own, garnished with some fresh basil leaves – or why not make a meal of it with a big salad and some oven baked wedges?

LIGHT BITES & LUNCHES

SWEET POTATO RÖSTI

These are a lovely vibrant orange and are perfect topped with whatever needs using up in the fridge – cheese, eggs, leftover cold meats . . . the list is endless!

Prep: 10 minutes | **Makes:** 4

750g sweet potatoes, peeled and grated

1 red onion, grated

2 tsp frozen chopped garlic

1 tsp salt

2 eggs

2 heaped tbsp plain flour

a good grind of black pepper

To cook:
olive oil

 ## IF MAKING AHEAD TO FREEZE

1 Put the grated sweet potato and red onion in the centre of a clean tea towel and squeeze out as much liquid as you can over the sink.

2 Place the grated potato and onion in a mixing bowl with the garlic, salt, eggs, flour and a good grind of black pepper, and stir to combine.

3 Using your hands, form the mix into 4 patties, firmly squishing them down into a circle shape that is around 1cm in thickness and placing them on individual squares of baking parchment.

4 Put the rösti on a tray and place in the freezer to flash freeze for 2 hours. After 2 hours, stack them on top of each other in a freezer bag and put back in the freezer, making sure the bag is well sealed.

 HOB

Heat a good glug of olive oil in a non-stick frying pan on a medium-high heat. Once hot, fry the frozen rösti for 4–5 minutes on each side, until golden and crispy.

OVEN

Preheat the oven to 190°C. Place the frozen rösti on a baking tray, keeping them on their baking parchment. Drizzle them with olive oil and cook for 30–35 minutes, until golden.

 AIR FRYER

Preheat the air fryer to 180°C. Keeping the frozen rösti on their baking parchment, drizzle each one with olive oil and cook for 15 minutes, then flip them over, peel off the parchment and cook for a further 10–12 minutes, until golden.

 ## IF COOKING NOW

Follow the method in the 'making ahead to freeze' section up until the end of step 3.

 HOB

Heat a good glug of olive oil in a non-stick frying pan on a medium-high heat. Once hot, fry the rösti for 3–5 minutes on each side, until golden and crispy.

OVEN

Preheat the oven to 190°C. Place the rösti on a baking tray, keeping them on their baking parchment. Drizzle with olive oil and cook for 25–30 minutes, until golden.

 AIR FRYER

Preheat the air fryer to 180°C. Keeping the rösti on their baking parchment, drizzle each one with olive oil and cook for 10 minutes, then flip them over, peel off the parchment and cook for a further 10 minutes, until golden.

TIP
I love to serve these with a fried egg and some spinach.

TURMERIC, LENTIL & SQUASH SOUP

I love a good easy soup recipe, and this is so tasty and beautifully spiced with turmeric, as well as being packed full of goodness.

Prep: 5 minutes | **Serves:** 4

1 cup (115g) frozen diced onions

2 tsp frozen chopped garlic

2 tsp frozen chopped ginger

2 tbsp frozen chopped coriander

2 cups (300g) frozen butternut squash chunks

⅔ cup (135g) dried red lentils, rinsed well

1 tsp ground turmeric

1 tsp mild chilli powder

1 vegetable stock cube, crumbled

To cook:
1 tbsp olive oil
(if cooking on hob or in pressure cooker)

5 cups (1.2 litres) boiling water

salt and pepper

❄ IF MAKING AHEAD TO FREEZE

Put all the ingredients into a large labelled freezer bag and mix. Before freezing, use the divided freezing method on pages 21–22 to ensure your frozen meal will fit into your pot or slow cooker. Seal and freeze flat.

🍳 HOB

When ready to cook, put 1 tablespoon of olive oil into a large saucepan. Place on the heat and tip in the bag of frozen soup mix. Cover with the boiling water, bring to the boil, then reduce the heat to a simmer and put a lid on the pan. Cook for 35 minutes, until all the vegetables are tender. Blend with a stick blender and season with salt and pepper to taste.

SLOW COOKER

Tip the bag of frozen soup mix into the slow cooker and cover with the boiling water. Put the lid on and cook for 4 hours on high, or 8 hours on low, until all the vegetables are tender. Once cooked, blend with a stick blender and season with salt and pepper to taste.

PRESSURE COOKER

Put 1 tablespoon of olive oil into the pressure cooker and tip in the frozen soup mix. Use the sauté setting and cook for 2–3 minutes, to allow everything to start to defrost. Cover with the boiling water and seal the lid. Cook for 18 minutes on the high pressure setting. Allow it to naturally release, then blend the soup with a stick blender and season with salt and pepper to taste.

🍲 IF COOKING NOW

🍳 HOB

Put 1 tablespoon of olive oil into a large saucepan. Place on the heat and tip in all the soup ingredients. Cover with the boiling water, stir, bring to the boil, then reduce the heat to a simmer and cover with a lid. Cook for 25–30 minutes, until all the vegetables are tender. Once cooked, blend with a stick blender and season with salt and pepper to taste.

SLOW COOKER

Put all the soup ingredients into the slow cooker, cover with the boiling water and stir. Put the lid on and cook for 3 hours on high, or 6 hours on low, until all the vegetables are tender. Once cooked, blend with a stick blender and season with salt and pepper to taste.

PRESSURE COOKER

Put 1 tablespoon of olive oil into the pressure cooker and add all the soup ingredients. Use the sauté setting and cook for 2–3 minutes. Cover with the boiling water and seal the lid. Cook for 15 minutes on the high pressure setting. Allow it to naturally release, then blend the soup with a stick blender and season with salt and pepper to taste.

TIP
Serve with some crusty bread and butter (use plant-based if cooking for vegans).

CHEESE, HAM & SWEETCORN TARTS

These little tarts are so easy and are great to have in the freezer for the perfect kiddy-friendly lunch! They're individually portioned for the freezer, so you can grab and cook as many as you need.

Prep: 5–10 minutes | **Makes:** 8

1 sheet of pre-rolled puff pastry

8 heaped tsp cream cheese

¾ cup (105g) grated Cheddar

3 slices of ham, finely chopped

1 cup (105g) drained tinned sweetcorn

1 egg, beaten

IF MAKING AHEAD TO FREEZE

1. Unroll the puff pastry sheet. Keeping it on its paper, cut it in half lengthways, then slice it into 8 rectangles.
2. Lightly score a border 1cm in from the edge of each rectangle.
3. Spread 1 heaped teaspoon of cream cheese on each rectangle, keeping inside the scored lines. Sprinkle over the grated cheese.
4. Divide the ham and sweetcorn between the 8 tarts.
5. Brush each pastry border with beaten egg to glaze.
6. Open your large labelled freezer bag. Keeping the bag flat, put in the tarts, lifting them off the paper, leaving space so they don't stick together. If you need to stack them on top of each other, add a sheet of baking parchment in between to stop them sticking together. Place flat in the freezer until fully frozen.

 OVEN

Preheat the oven to 180°C. Slide the frozen tarts onto a lined baking tray and cook them for 20–25 minutes, until golden and crisp.

 AIR FRYER

Preheat the air fryer to 180°C. Slide in the frozen tarts and cook them for 10–12 minutes, until golden and crisp.

IF COOKING NOW

Follow the method in the 'making ahead to freeze' section up until the end of step 5.

 OVEN

Preheat the oven to 180°C. Slide the tarts, still on the paper, onto a baking tray and cook them for 15–20 minutes, until golden and crisp.

 AIR FRYER

Preheat the air fryer to 180°C. Slide in the tarts and cook them for 9–10 minutes, until golden and crisp.

TIP
Serve with a big green salad, or make into a full meal with a side of oven chips.

LIGHT BITES & LUNCHES

LAMB, FETA & HARISSA SAUSAGE ROLLS

These sausage rolls are such a wonderful combination of flavours. Super easy to make and so moreish! Not a fan of lamb? Simply change it up to pork mince.

Prep: 15 minutes | **Makes:** 16

400g lamb mince

100g feta cheese, crumbled

3 heaped tsp harissa paste

1 tsp ground cumin

salt and pepper

1 sheet of pre-rolled puff pastry

1 egg, beaten

sesame seeds, to sprinkle over the top

❄ IF MAKING AHEAD TO FREEZE

1 Put the lamb mince, feta cheese, harissa paste and cumin into a mixing bowl and season with salt and pepper. Mix with your hands.

2 Unroll the puff pastry, keeping it on its paper, and cut it in half lengthways.

3 Divide the meat in two and lay down the middle of each length of pastry.

4 Lightly brush the beaten egg down one side of each length of pastry.

5 Fold the other side of the pastry over to meet the egg-washed edge and enclose the meat. Go around the edges with a fork to make sure they are well sealed.

6 Slice each length into 8, giving you 16 sausage rolls. Brush the tops with egg and sprinkle with sesame seeds.

7 Open your large labelled freezer bag. Keeping it flat, lift the sausage rolls off the paper and put them in, leaving space so they don't stick together. If you need to stack them on top of each other, add some parchment in between to stop them sticking. Place flat in the freezer until fully frozen.

🔲 OVEN

Preheat the oven to 190°C. Place the frozen sausage rolls on a lined baking tray and cook for 30–35 minutes, until golden and puffed.

🔲 AIR FRYER

Preheat the air fryer to 185°C. Cook the frozen sausage rolls in the air fryer for 20 minutes, until golden and puffed.

🍲 IF COOKING NOW

Follow the method in the 'making ahead to freeze' section up until the end of step 6.

🔲 OVEN

Preheat the oven to 190°C. Place the sausage rolls on a lined baking tray and cook for 25–30 minutes, until golden and puffed.

🔲 AIR FRYER

Preheat the air fryer to 185°C. Cook the sausage rolls in the air fryer for 15 minutes, until golden and puffed.

TIP
To make this vegetarian, use plant-based mince.

FRENCH ONION SOUP

This classic French soup is such a comforting bowl. There are quite a few onions to slice, but I promise it is worth it!

Prep: 10 minutes | **Serves:** 4

1kg onions, finely sliced

3 tsp frozen chopped garlic

1 tbsp caster sugar

1 tsp salt

2 tbsp plain flour

1 beef stock cube, crumbled

2 bay leaves

½ tsp dried thyme

To cook:
40g butter

6¼ cups (1.5 litres) boiling water

 IF MAKING AHEAD TO FREEZE

Put the sliced onions into a large labelled freezer bag. Put everything else into a smaller freezer bag. Place the small freezer bag inside the large bag of onions and freeze flat.

HOB

Place a large saucepan on the hob and add the butter. Once melted, add the frozen onions and cook down on a low heat for 45–50 minutes, stirring regularly, until soft and caramelised. Tip in the smaller bag of frozen ingredients and stir through. Cook for 1 minute, then add the boiling water. Bring to the boil, then reduce the heat to a simmer for 15 minutes before serving.

SLOW COOKER

Turn the slow cooker on high and add the butter. Once melted, add the frozen onions, close the lid and cook for 4 hours on high, stirring every hour, until soft and caramelised. Stir through the smaller bag of frozen ingredients, then pour over the boiling water, close the lid and cook for a further 2 hours on low before serving.

PRESSURE COOKER

Turn the pressure cooker on to the sauté setting. Add the butter and melt, then add the frozen onions and sauté for 35–45 minutes, stirring often, until soft and caramelised. Stir through the smaller bag of frozen ingredients, cook for 1 minute, then add the boiling water. Stir well, then seal the lid and cook on high pressure for 6 minutes, allowing it to naturally release for at least 15 minutes before serving.

 IF COOKING NOW

HOB

Place a large saucepan on the hob and add the butter. Once melted, add the sliced onions and cook down on a low heat for 35–45 minutes, stirring often, until soft and caramelised. Add the rest of the ingredients and stir through the onions. Cook for 1 minute, then add the boiling water. Bring to the boil, then reduce the heat to a simmer for 15 minutes before serving.

SLOW COOKER

Turn the slow cooker on high and add the butter. Once melted, add the sliced onions, close the lid and cook for 3 hours on high, stirring every hour, until soft and caramelised. Stir through the rest of the ingredients, then pour over the boiling water, close the lid and cook for a further 2 hours on low before serving.

PRESSURE COOKER

Turn the pressure cooker on to the sauté setting. Add the butter and melt, then add the onions and sauté for 30–35 minutes, until soft and caramelised, stirring often. Once caramelised, stir through everything else, then add the boiling water. Stir well, then seal the lid and cook on high pressure for 8 minutes, allowing it to naturally release for 15 minutes before serving.

TIP
Serve with crusty bread topped with melted Gruyère cheese, and lots of black pepper.

67

PIZZA OPEN BAGELS

These are the perfect after-school snack and are brilliant to have in the freezer for when the craving for a bite strikes! They are topped with mozzarella and pepperoni, but feel free to get creative and add any other toppings you like!

Prep: 5 minutes | **Serves:** 4

8 tbsp pizza sauce

4 bagels, halved

1 large ball of mozzarella, drained and torn into pieces

32 small slices of pepperoni

 IF MAKING AHEAD TO FREEZE

1 Spread 1 tablespoon of pizza sauce over each half bagel.

2 Scatter the torn mozzarella over all the halves and top each one with 4 slices of pepperoni.

3 Wrap each half bagel in cling film or foil, then place in a large labelled freezer bag and freeze flat.

 OVEN

Preheat the oven to 180°C. Unwrap the frozen bagel halves, place them on a lined baking tray, topping side up, and cook for 9–10 minutes, until lovely and bubbling.

 AIR FRYER

Preheat the air fryer to 180°C. Cook the frozen bagel halves, topping side up, for 5–7 minutes, until lovely and bubbling.

 IF COOKING NOW

Follow the method in the 'making ahead to freeze' section up until the end of step 2.

 OVEN

Preheat the grill. Put the bagel halves on a baking tray, topping side up, and grill for 6–8 minutes, until lovely and bubbling.

AIR FRYER

Preheat the air fryer to 180°C. Cook the bagel halves, topping side up, for 3–4 minutes, until lovely and bubbling.

TIP

Serve the bagels as they are, garnished with fresh basil, or make them into a full meal with potato wedges and a salad.

TORTELLINI SOUP

This delicious Italian-style soup makes the perfect warming lunch. The tortellini pasta is such a brilliant addition, and really fills you up!

Prep: 5 minutes | **Serves:** 4

1 cup (115g) frozen diced onions

2 tsp frozen chopped garlic

1 large carrot, peeled and finely diced

1 x 400g tin of chopped tomatoes

a large handful of fresh basil, roughly chopped

1 vegetable stock cube, crumbled

2 tbsp cream cheese

1 x 300g pack of spinach and ricotta tortellini

To cook:

a splash of oil (*if cooking on hob or in pressure cooker*)

3½ cups (850ml) boiling water

TIP

I like to serve this with lots of Parmesan (or a vegetarian alternative) and some buttered crusty bread.

 IF MAKING AHEAD TO FREEZE

1 Mix all the ingredients except the tortellini in a large labelled freezer bag.
2 Before freezing, use the divided freezing method on pages 21–22 to make sure that your frozen meal will fit into your pot or slow cooker.
3 Freeze flat, with the pack of tortellini alongside it.

 HOB

Put a splash of oil into a large saucepan and tip in the contents of the freezer bag. Stir to break everything up, then add the boiling water. Bring to the boil, then reduce to a simmer. After 25 minutes, add the frozen tortellini and cook for 7–8 minutes, until the tortellini are cooked through.

 SLOW COOKER

Tip the contents of the freezer bag into the slow cooker and cover with the boiling water. Stir to break everything up, then pop the lid on and cook for 3 hours on high, or 6 hours on low. An hour before the end of the cooking time, add the tortellini.

PRESSURE COOKER

Put a splash of oil into the pressure cooker, then tip in everything apart from the tortellini and turn it to the sauté setting. Add the boiling water, stir, then seal the lid and cook on high pressure for 8 minutes. Allow to naturally release for 5 minutes, then open up and add the tortellini. Turn to the sauté setting and cook for around 7–8 minutes, until the tortellini are cooked.

 IF COOKING NOW

 HOB

Put a splash of oil into a large saucepan and add everything apart from the tortellini. Stir well, then add the boiling water. Bring to the boil, then reduce to a simmer. After 20 minutes, add the tortellini and cook for a further 5–6 minutes, until the tortellini are cooked through.

 SLOW COOKER

Put everything into the slow cooker apart from the tortellini and cover with the boiling water. Stir, then pop the lid on and cook for 3 hours on high, or 6 hours on low. An hour before the end of the cooking time, add the tortellini.

PRESSURE COOKER

Put a splash of oil into the pressure cooker, then tip in everything apart from the tortellini and turn it to the sauté setting. Add the boiling water, stir, seal the lid and cook on high pressure for 8 minutes. Allow to naturally release for 5 minutes, then open up and add the tortellini. Turn to the sauté setting and cook for 5–6 minutes, until the tortellini are cooked through.

CLASSIC POTATO RÖSTI

Rösti are such a great easy lunch option. They are perfect for topping with whatever needs using up in the fridge – cheese, eggs, leftover cold meats . . . the list is endless!

Prep: 5–10 minutes | **Makes:** 4

750g potatoes, peeled and grated

1 onion, grated

2 tsp frozen chopped garlic

1 tsp salt

2 eggs, beaten

2 heaped tbsp plain flour

a good grind of black pepper

To cook:
olive oil

 ## IF MAKING AHEAD TO FREEZE

1 Put the grated potato and onion in the centre of a clean tea towel and squeeze out as much liquid as you can over the sink.
2 Put the potato and onion into a mixing bowl along with the garlic, salt, eggs, flour and a good grind of black pepper, and stir to combine.
3 Using your hands, form into 4 patties, firmly squishing them down into a circle shape around 1cm in thickness, and placing them on individual squares of baking parchment.
4 Put the rösti on a tray and place in the freezer to flash freeze for 2 hours. After 2 hours, stack them on top of each other in a freezer bag and put back into the freezer, making sure the bag is well sealed.

 ### HOB

Heat a good glug of olive oil in a non-stick frying pan on a medium-high heat. Once hot, fry the frozen rösti for 4–5 minutes on each side, until golden and crispy.

OVEN

Preheat the oven to 190°C. Place the frozen rösti on a baking tray, keeping them on their baking parchment. Drizzle with olive oil and cook them for 30–35 minutes, until golden.

 ### AIR FRYER

Preheat the air fryer to 180°C. Keeping the frozen rösti on their baking parchment, drizzle each one with olive oil and cook for 15 minutes, then flip them over, peel off the parchment and cook for a further 10–12 minutes, until golden.

IF COOKING NOW

Follow the method in the 'making ahead to freeze' section up until the end of step 3.

 ### HOB

Heat a good glug of olive oil in a non-stick frying pan on a medium-high heat. Once hot, fry the rösti for 3–5 minutes on each side, until golden and crispy.

OVEN

Preheat the oven to 190°C. Place the rösti on a baking tray, keeping them on their baking parchment. Drizzle with olive oil and cook them for 25–30 minutes, until golden.

AIR FRYER

Preheat the air fryer to 180°C. Keeping the rosti on their baking parchment, drizzle with olive oil and cook for 10 minutes, then flip them over, peel off the baking parchment and cook for 10 minutes, until golden.

 TIP

I love to serve these with chilli jam, a fried egg and grilled or baked tomatoes.

MOROCCAN-SPICED HUMMUS

Hummus is such an easy thing to make at home. This dip brings delicious flavours of the Middle East, with lovely warming spices. I love it as a healthy lunch with pitta bread and crunchy vegetables. Grab your blender and let's go!

Prep: 5 minutes | **Serves:** 4

1 x 400g tin of chickpeas

2 tbsp tahini

1 tsp frozen chopped garlic

juice of 1 lemon

1 tsp ground cumin

1 tsp ground coriander

½ tsp smoked paprika

a pinch of ground cinnamon

2 tbsp olive oil

salt and pepper

 IF MAKING AHEAD TO FREEZE

1 Drain the chickpeas, reserving half a cup (120ml) of the liquid.
2 Put the chickpeas into a blender with the tahini, garlic, lemon juice, cumin, coriander, smoked paprika, cinnamon and olive oil. Season with salt and pepper and add a good splash of the chickpea liquid. Blitz, adding more chickpea liquid if the hummus is too thick. It should be spoonable.
3 Spoon into a labelled freezer bag or into an ice cube tray so that you can pop out single portions as and when you want.

READY TO EAT

Remove the hummus from the freezer and allow it to fully defrost. Once defrosted, use the hummus as you like.

 IF MAKING NOW

Follow the method in the 'making ahead to freeze' section up until the end of step 2. Leave the hummus to sit for 30 minutes before eating for the flavours to develop.

FETA & SPINACH FILO SWIRLS

If you have ever been to Greece you have likely tried spanakopita, and these swirls are my take on it. Grab your tin of cooked spinach purée from the world food aisle in your local supermarket, or use frozen chopped spinach, and give these cheesy, crunchy swirls a go!

Prep: 10 minutes | **Makes:** 8

800g tinned spinach purée, or 30 cubes of frozen chopped spinach (roughly 800g), defrosted

a large handful of fresh parsley, finely chopped

a large handful of fresh dill, finely chopped

200g feta cheese, crumbled

1 egg, beaten

1 tsp salt

a good grind of black pepper

1 pack of filo pastry (you will need 8 sheets)

3 tbsp olive oil

 ## IF MAKING AHEAD TO FREEZE

1 Put the spinach in a clean tea towel and squeeze out as much liquid as you can.
2 Place the drained spinach in a mixing bowl with the parsley, dill, feta and egg. Add the salt and pepper and mix well.
3 Lay one sheet of filo pastry on your work surface and brush it all over with olive oil. Keep the other sheets of filo under a damp tea towel to stop them drying out.
4 Add ⅛ of the filling in a line along the bottom of the filo sheet, just in from the edge, then loosely roll up the

pastry into a long sausage shape. Coil it round carefully to create a spiral, making sure not to roll it too tight, otherwise the pastry may break. Brush the swirl well with olive oil. Repeat to make the other 7 swirls.
5 Open your large labelled freezer bag. Keeping the bag flat, put in the swirls, leaving space so they don't stick together. If stacking them on top of each other, add a layer of baking parchment to stop them sticking and place flat in the freezer until fully frozen.

OVEN

Preheat the oven to 180°C. Place the frozen swirls on a lined baking tray and cook for 22–25 minutes, until golden.

AIR FRYER

Preheat the air fryer to 180°C. Put the frozen swirls on some baking parchment and cook for 12–14 minutes, flipping over halfway through, until golden.

IF COOKING NOW

Follow the method in the 'making ahead to freeze' section up until the end of step 4.

OVEN

Preheat the oven to 180°C. Place the swirls on a lined baking tray and cook for 20–22 minutes, until golden.

AIR FRYER

Preheat the air fryer to 180°C. Place the swirls on baking parchment and cook for 12 minutes, flipping over halfway through, until golden.

TIP
Serve with a lovely side salad and some tzatziki.

SMOKED MACKEREL PÂTÉ

Smoked mackerel pâté is perfect for a picnic lunch, an easy canapé or a starter!
Spread on bread, or scoop with crackers!

Prep: 5 minutes | **Serves:** 4

1 x 200g pack of cooked
boneless peppered
mackerel fillets, skin
removed

2 heaped tbsp cream
cheese

1 heaped tbsp creamed
horseradish

zest and juice of 1 lemon

a handful of fresh parsley

 IF MAKING AHEAD TO FREEZE

1 Blend the mackerel, cream cheese,
   horseradish, lemon zest and juice and
   the parsley until smooth.

2 Spoon the pâté into a labelled freezer
   bag and freeze flat.

READY TO EAT

Remove from the freezer and leave to fully defrost. Once defrosted, use the pâté as
you like.

 IF MAKING NOW

Follow the method in the 'making ahead to freeze' section up until the end of step 1.
The pâté is now ready to be used however you like. It will keep in an airtight container
in the fridge for up to 3 days.

LIGHT BITES & LUNCHES

GOAT'S CHEESE & CARAMELISED ONION CANNONCINI

Goat's cheese and caramelised onion is one of my favourite combinations. This filling, rolled in pastry, creates a taste sensation that would brighten up any lunchtime.

Prep: 5–10 minutes | **Makes:** 6

1 sheet of pre-rolled puff pastry

6 tbsp caramelised onion chutney

150g goat's cheese log, cut into 12 slices

1 tsp dried thyme

1 egg, beaten

TIP

I also like to make Pesto, Olive & Mozzarella Cannoncini. Instead of caramelised onion chutney, goat's cheese and dried thyme, use 6 tablespoons of basil pesto, ¾ cup (105g) grated mozzarella and 16 pitted mixed olives. In step 3, spread 1 tablespoon of pesto on the uncut half of the square and add a hand-ful of mozzarella cheese and some chopped olives. Continue with the recipe from step 4.

 IF MAKING AHEAD TO FREEZE

1 Unroll the sheet of puff pastry and cut it into 6 squares.
2 On each square, lightly score down the middle. On the right-hand side, cut long thin strips from the middle to the edge using a sharp knife.
3 Spread 1 tablespoon of chutney on the uncut half of the square and add 2 slices of goat's cheese and a sprinkle of thyme.

4 Roll up the filling side over the strips side, then tuck in the edges and repeat until you have 6 cannoncini rolls. Brush all over with the beaten egg.
5 Open your large labelled freezer bag. Keeping the bag flat, put in the pastries, leaving space so they don't stick together. Place flat in the freezer until fully frozen.

OVEN

Preheat the oven to 180°C. Slide the frozen cannoncini onto a lined baking tray and cook for 35–40 minutes, until golden.

AIR FRYER

Preheat the air fryer to 180°C. Slide in the frozen cannoncini and cook for 18–20 minutes, until golden.

 IF COOKING NOW

Follow the method in the 'making ahead to freeze' section up until the end of step 4.

OVEN

Preheat the oven to 180°C. Slide the cannoncini onto a lined baking tray and cook for 25–30 minutes, until golden.

AIR FRYER

Preheat the air fryer to 180°C. Slide in the cannoncini and cook for 15 minutes, until golden.

HAM, CHEESE & DIJON FOLDED SQUARES

These are seriously easy to make and are great to have in the freezer for quick, easy lunches! I love them. If I am making them for the kids, I often swap the Dijon for sun-dried tomato pesto.

Prep: 10 minutes | **Makes:** 6

1 sheet of pre-rolled puff pastry

2 tbsp Dijon mustard

6 slices of ham, cut in half

¾ cup (105g) grated cheese

1 egg, beaten

TIP

I also like to make Cheesy Pepperoni Folded Squares. Instead of Dijon mustard and ham, use 6 tablespoons of pizza sauce, 18 slices of pepperoni, 12 fresh basil leaves and the same amount of cheese as above. In step 2, spread 1 tablespoon of pizza sauce instead of mustard, then add 3 slices of pepperoni, a sprinkle of grated cheese and a couple of basil leaves to each square. Continue with the recipe from step 3.

❄ IF MAKING AHEAD TO FREEZE

1   Unroll the sheet of puff pastry and cut it into 6 squares.
2   Spread a little Dijon mustard over each square, across the diagonal. Layer 2 half slices of ham on each square and sprinkle over the grated cheese.
3   Fold one of the corners into the centre, brush with a little beaten egg, then fold the opposite corner in to meet the pastry – the egg will help it to stick. Brush all the exposed pastry with beaten egg.
4   Open your large labelled freezer bag. Keeping the bag flat, put in the pastries, leaving space so they don't stick together. If you need to stack them on top of each other, add a sheet of baking parchment to stop them sticking together. Place flat in the freezer until fully frozen.

▢ OVEN

Preheat the oven to 180°C. Slide the frozen pastries onto a lined baking tray and cook for 22–25 minutes, until golden and crisp.

AIR FRYER

Preheat the air fryer to 180°C. Slide in the frozen pastries and cook for 13 minutes, until golden and crisp.

🍲 IF COOKING NOW

Follow the method in the 'making ahead to freeze' section up until the end of step 3.

▢ OVEN

Preheat the oven to 180°C. Slide the pastries onto a lined baking tray and cook for 20–25 minutes, until golden and crisp.

AIR FRYER

Preheat the air fryer to 180°C. Slide in the pastries and cook for 10–11 minutes, until golden and crisp.

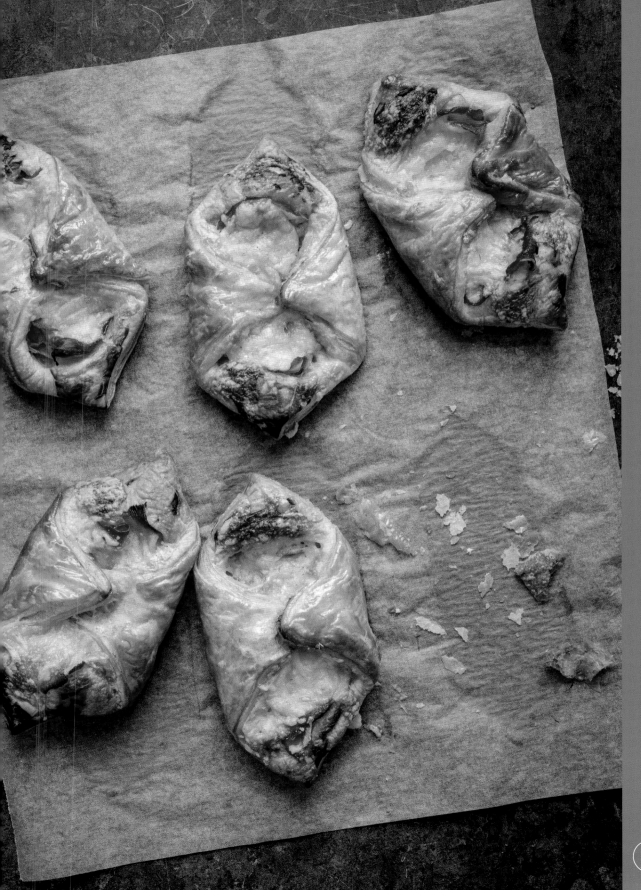

MEXICAN-SPICED CORN CHOWDER

This is a super delicious Mexican-inspired soup! It's zingy, fresh, creamy, and everything you could want from a bowl of soup. If you love sweetcorn, this is for you!

Prep: 5 minutes | **Serves:** 4–6

1 cup (115g) frozen diced onions

2 tsp frozen chopped garlic

1 x 325g tin of sweetcorn, drained

1 x 567g tin of potatoes, drained and cut into chunks

1 red pepper, deseeded and finely diced

1 tsp chilli powder

1 tsp smoked paprika

juice of 1 lime

a large handful of fresh coriander, chopped

1 vegetable stock cube, crumbled

salt and pepper

To cook:

1 tbsp olive oil (*if cooking on hob or in pressure cooker*)

5 cups (1.2 litres) boiling water

1 heaped tbsp crème fraîche

TIP

I love to serve this with some chopped fresh coriander, a swirl of crème fraîche and tortilla crisps.

 IF MAKING AHEAD TO FREEZE

1 Put all the ingredients into a large labelled freezer bag, adding to the label that you will need 1 tablespoon of crème fraîche when you come to cook.

2 Before freezing, use the divided freezing method on pages 21–22 to ensure your meal will fit into your pot or slow cooker. Seal and freeze flat.

 HOB

Put 1 tablespoon of olive oil into a large saucepan and place on a medium heat. Add all the frozen ingredients and sauté for 2–3 minutes, then cover with the boiling water. Bring to the boil, reduce to a simmer and cook for 25 minutes, until soft. Remove from the heat, add a heaped spoonful of crème fraîche and blend with a stick blender.

SLOW COOKER

Put all the frozen ingredients into the slow cooker, cover with the boiling water, pop the lid on and cook for 4 hours on high, or 8 hours on low. Once cooked, add a heaped spoonful of crème fraîche and blend with a stick blender.

PRESSURE COOKER

Put 1 tablespoon of olive oil into the pressure cooker and turn to the sauté setting. Add all the frozen ingredients and sauté for 2–3 minutes, then cover with the boiling water. Seal the lid and cook for 10 minutes on high pressure, then allow it to naturally release. Add a heaped spoonful of crème fraîche and blend with a stick blender.

 IF COOKING NOW

 **HOB**

Put 1 tablespoon of olive oil into a large saucepan and place on a medium heat. Put all the ingredients into the saucepan and sauté for 2–3 minutes, then cover with the boiling water. Bring to the boil, reduce to a simmer and cook for 20 minutes, until soft. Once cooked, remove from the heat, add a heaped spoonful of crème fraîche and blend with a stick blender.

SLOW COOKER

Put all the ingredients into the slow cooker, cover with the boiling water, pop the lid on, and cook for 3 hours on high, or 6 hours on low. Once cooked, add a heaped spoonful of crème fraîche and blend with a stick blender.

PRESSURE COOKER

Put 1 tablespoon of olive oil into the pressure cooker. Turn to the sauté setting and add the rest of the ingredients. Sauté for 2–3 minutes, then cover with the boiling water. Seal the lid and cook on high pressure for 10 minutes, then allow it to naturally release. Once cooked, add a heaped spoonful of crème fraîche and blend with a stick blender.

PORK, BLACK PUDDING & APPLE SAUSAGE ROLLS

These sausage rolls are a delicious variation on the traditional ones. Black pudding is a real favourite of mine and if you haven't given it a go, I would really recommend it.

Prep: 15 minutes | **Makes:** 16

300g pork sausage meat

100g black pudding, outer casing removed

1 eating apple, cored and grated

salt and pepper

1 sheet of pre-rolled puff pastry

1 egg, beaten

sesame seeds, to sprinkle over the top

 IF MAKING AHEAD TO FREEZE

1 Put the sausage meat into a mixing bowl, crumble in the black pudding and add the grated apple. Season with salt and pepper, then mix well, using your hands so the black pudding and apple is well distributed.
2 Unroll the puff pastry, keeping it on its paper, and cut it in half lengthways.
3 Divide the meat in two and lay down the middle of each length of pastry.
4 Lightly brush some beaten egg down one side of each length of pastry.
5 Now fold the other side of the pastry over to meet the egg-washed edge.

Go around the edges with a fork to make sure they are well sealed.
6 Slice each length into 8, giving you 16 sausage rolls. Brush the tops with egg and sprinkle with sesame seeds.
7 Open your large labelled freezer bag. Keeping it flat, lift the sausage rolls off the paper and put them in, leaving space so they don't stick together. If you need to stack on top of each other, add a layer of baking parchment in between to stop them sticking together. Place flat in the freezer until fully frozen.

 OVEN

Preheat the oven to 190°C and place the frozen sausage rolls on a lined baking tray. Cook for 30–35 minutes, until golden and puffed.

 AIR FRYER

Preheat the air fryer to 185°C. Cook the frozen sausage rolls for 20 minutes, until golden and puffed.

 IF COOKING NOW

Follow the method in the 'making ahead to freeze' section up until the end of step 6.

OVEN

Preheat the oven to 190°C and place the sausage rolls on a lined baking tray. Cook for 25–30 minutes, until golden and puffed.

AIR FRYER

Preheat the air fryer to 185°C. Cook the sausage rolls for 15 minutes, until golden and puffed.

SAMOSA-STYLE BITES

These super easy samosas are a great lunch option and such fun to make! The leftover tinned chickpeas are good stirred through some rice for an easy side dish.

Prep: 15 minutes | **Makes:** 12

1 x 215g tin of chickpeas, drained and rinsed

1 small carrot, peeled and grated

3 spring onions, finely chopped

2 tsp frozen chopped garlic

1 tbsp mango chutney

1 tbsp curry powder

½ tsp mild chilli powder

salt and pepper

3 sheets of filo pastry

2–3 tbsp vegetable oil

❄️ IF MAKING AHEAD TO FREEZE

1 Put the drained chickpeas into a mixing bowl and squash them with a fork until you have a rough paste.
2 Add the carrot, spring onions, garlic, mango chutney, curry powder and chilli powder. Mix well and season with salt and pepper.
3 Lay out the 3 sheets of filo pastry on top of each other on a work surface. Using a knife, cut the layers of filo into 4 long strips.
4 Place 1 heaped teaspoon of the filling in the top left hand of the first filo strip, being sure to only pick up 1 strip. Fold the top left-hand corner over and continue to fold into a triangle shape. When you get to the end, brush the samosa with oil to stick the last corner so you have a nice neat triangle. Repeat with the rest of the filling mix and filo strips.
5 Brush each samosa all over with oil.
6 Open your large labelled freezer bag. Keeping the bag flat, put in the samosas, leaving space so they don't stick together. If you need to stack them on top of each other, add a layer of baking parchment in between to stop them sticking together. Place flat in the freezer until fully frozen.

🍳 OVEN

Preheat the oven to 180°C. Slide the frozen samosas onto a lined baking tray and cook for 18–20 minutes, until golden.

🍟 AIR FRYER

Preheat the air fryer to 180°C. Slide in the frozen samosas and cook for 12–14 minutes, flipping them over halfway through and cooking until golden.

🍲 IF COOKING NOW

Follow the method in the 'making ahead to freeze' section up until the end of step 5.

🍳 OVEN

Preheat the oven to 180°C. Slide the samosas onto a lined baking tray and cook for 15–20 minutes, until golden.

🍟 AIR FRYER

Preheat the air fryer to 180°C. Slide in the samosas and cook for 12 minutes, flipping them over halfway through and cooking until golden.

TIP

Serve with mango chutney on the side.

WEEKNIGHT

BOMBAY FISH FINGERS

If you love Bombay mix, these super easy fish fingers are for you! These are a fun twist on one of the nation's favourites, using this Indian snack as the crumb coating instead of the traditional breadcrumbs. You can use any white fish you like – cod or coley work great.

Prep: 10 minutes | **Serves:** 4

1½ cups (150g) Bombay mix

½ cup (55g) plain flour

2 eggs, beaten

salt and pepper

400g skinless cod or coley fillets, cut into 12 slices/fingers

To cook:

vegetable oil, to drizzle

 IF MAKING AHEAD TO FREEZE

1 Put the Bombay mix into a food processor and blitz until you have crumbs. You can also do this by putting them into a freezer bag and bashing them with a rolling pin.
2 Take three shallow bowls and put the Bombay crumbs into one, the flour into another and the eggs into a third. Season the flour and eggs, then line up the bowls – flour, eggs, then crumbs.
3 Take a slice of fish and dip it first into the flour, then into the egg and then into the Bombay crumbs, making sure to coat well at each stage. Repeat with the rest of the fish slices.
4 Open your large labelled freezer bag. Keeping the bag flat, put in the fish fingers, leaving space so they don't stick together. If stacking them on top of each other, add a layer of baking parchment to stop them sticking together. Place flat in the freezer until fully frozen.

 OVEN

Preheat the oven to 180°C. Drizzle the frozen fish fingers with a little oil and cook on a lined baking tray for 30 minutes, until golden all over.

 AIR FRYER

Preheat the air fryer to 180°C. Drizzle the frozen fish fingers with a little oil and cook for 17–18 minutes, flipping them over halfway through, until golden all over.

 IF COOKING NOW

Follow the method in the 'making ahead to freeze' section up until the end of step 3.

 OVEN

Preheat the oven to 180°C. Place the fish fingers on a lined baking tray and drizzle with oil. Cook for 20 minutes, until golden all over.

 AIR FRYER

Preheat the air fryer to 180°C. Drizzle the fish fingers with oil and cook for 12–13 minutes, flipping them over halfway through, until golden all over.

 TIP

Serve in wraps, with lettuce, cucumber, mayonnaise and mango chutney.

GOAT'S CHEESE & SUN-DRIED TOMATO STUFFED CHICKEN BREASTS

I love the ease of a stuffed chicken breast, and this one is perfect! Creamy goat's cheese and sun-dried tomatoes go so well together – these will be your new midweek go-to!

Prep: 5 minutes | **Serves:** 4

1 x 150g log of soft goat's cheese

2 heaped tbsp cream cheese

12 sun-dried tomatoes in oil, drained and diced

1 tsp dried thyme

salt and pepper

4 skinless and boneless chicken breasts (approx. 160g each)

 IF MAKING AHEAD TO FREEZE

1 Mix the goat's cheese, cream cheese, sun-dried tomatoes, thyme and some salt and pepper in a small bowl.
2 Place the chicken breasts on a chopping board and cut down the side of each one to create a pocket, making sure you don't cut all the way through the breast.
3 Divide the goat's cheese mix between the pockets.
4 Put the stuffed chicken breasts into a labelled freezer bag and freeze flat.

 OVEN

Remove from the freezer and leave to fully defrost. Preheat the oven to 180°C. Place the chicken breasts on a lined baking tray and cook for 25–30 minutes, until the chicken is cooked through.

 AIR FRYER

Remove from the freezer and leave to fully defrost. Preheat the air fryer to 180°C. Place the chicken breasts in the air fryer and cook for 18–20 minutes, until the chicken is cooked through.

 IF COOKING NOW

Follow the method in the 'making ahead to freeze' section up until the end of step 3.

 OVEN

Preheat the oven to 180°C. Put the chicken breasts on a lined baking tray and cook for 25–30 minutes, until the chicken is cooked through.

AIR FRYER

Preheat the air fryer to 180°C. Put the chicken breasts into the air fryer and cook for 18–20 minutes, until the chicken is cooked through.

TIP
Serve with baked potatoes or herby couscous and a lovely green salad.

SALMON & NOODLE PARCELS

These Asian-inspired foil parcels are so delicious – fresh, zingy and packed full of flavour! This recipe uses pre-cooked straight-to-wok noodles – you will find these next to the rice and pasta section in the supermarket.

Prep: 10 minutes | **Serves:** 4

1 x 300g pack of cooked straight-to-wok medium noodles

250g pak choi, leaves pulled apart

4 salmon fillets (approx. 130g each)

4 tbsp soy sauce

2 tbsp sweet chilli sauce

2 tsp frozen chopped ginger

2 tsp frozen chopped garlic

juice of 1 lime

1 tbsp runny honey

1 tbsp Chinese rice vinegar

a large handful of fresh coriander, finely chopped

 IF MAKING AHEAD TO FREEZE

1 Cut 4 squares of tin foil, each roughly 35 x 30cm.
2 These noodles will be tightly packed, so remove them from the packet and pull them apart. Divide them between the tin foil squares, placing them in a pile in the centre of each one. Top each one with 2 or 3 leaves of pak choi.
3 Put the salmon fillets on top, then bring up the sides of the parcels, leaving them open at the top so you can pour the marinade in.

4 Mix the soy sauce, sweet chilli sauce, ginger, garlic, lime juice, honey and Chinese rice vinegar together in a bowl. Pour the marinade over the fish, dividing it evenly between the parcels, then sprinkle some chopped coriander over each fillet. Wrap the parcels up well, so they are completely sealed and no liquid can escape.
5 Place the parcels in a large labelled freezer bag and freeze flat.

 OVEN

Preheat the oven to 180°C. Place the frozen parcels on a baking tray and open them up slightly at the top. Cook for 30 minutes, until the salmon is cooked through.

 AIR FRYER

Preheat the air fryer to 180°C. Place the frozen parcels in the air fryer and open them up slightly at the top. Cook for 20–25 minutes, until the salmon is cooked through.

 IF COOKING NOW

Follow the method in the 'making ahead to freeze' section up until the end of step 4.

 OVEN

Preheat the oven to 180°C. Place the parcels on a baking tray and open them up slightly at the top. Cook for 20–25 minutes, until the salmon is cooked through.

 AIR FRYER

Preheat the air fryer to 180°C. Place the parcels inside and open them up slightly at the top. Cook for 14–16 minutes, until the salmon is cooked through.

CHICKEN SHAWARMA TRAYBAKE

If you love a chicken shawarma from the kebab house then this is right up your street, and half the price if you make it at home! This one-pan dish is packed full of juicy spiced chicken and veggies.

Prep: 5–10 minutes | **Serves:** 4

2 cloves of garlic, grated

1 tbsp ground coriander

1 tsp ground cumin

2 tsp paprika

juice of 1 lemon

4 tbsp olive oil

1 tsp salt

6–8 skinless and boneless chicken thighs

2 red peppers, deseeded and cut into thick strips

2 red onions, cut into thick chunks

300g frozen sweet potato chunks

 IF MAKING AHEAD TO FREEZE

1 Combine the grated garlic, the coriander, cumin, paprika, lemon juice, olive oil and salt in a large bowl and mix into a paste.

2 Add the chicken thighs, red peppers, red onions and sweet potato chunks and give everything a good mix.

3 Put into a large labelled freezer bag and freeze flat.

 OVEN

Remove from the freezer and leave to fully defrost. Preheat the oven to 180°C. Pour the mix into a large baking tray and arrange the chicken thighs so they are on top of the vegetables. Cook for 35 minutes, until golden and delicious.

AIR FRYER

Remove from the freezer and leave to fully defrost. Preheat the air fryer to 180°C. Pour the mix into an air fryer-safe dish and arrange the chicken thighs so they are on top. Cook for 25 minutes, until golden and delicious, giving everything a good shake halfway through, and turning the chicken over.

IF COOKING NOW

Follow the method in the 'making ahead to freeze' section up until the end of step 2.

 OVEN

Preheat the oven to 180°C. Pour the mix into a large baking tray and arrange the chicken thighs so they are on top of the vegetables. Cook for 35 minutes, until golden and delicious.

AIR FRYER

Preheat the air fryer to 180°C. Pour the mix into an air fryer-safe dish and arrange the chicken thighs so they are on top. Cook for 25 minutes, until golden and delicious, giving everything a good shake halfway through, and turning the chicken over.

TIP
Serve with chopped fresh coriander and a dollop of yoghurt.

BEEF RAGÙ

If you love spaghetti bolognese, this beef ragù recipe is for you! With similar flavours to a bolognese, ragù uses diced beef which is slow-cooked, making the most delicious and melt-in-the-mouth pasta sauce.

Prep: 5 minutes | **Serves:** 4

1 cup (115g) frozen diced onions

2 tsp frozen chopped garlic

1 large carrot, peeled and finely diced

2 celery sticks, finely diced

2 tbsp tomato purée

2 bay leaves

1 beef stock cube, crumbled

salt and pepper

2 cups (500ml) passata

½ cup (120ml) red wine

750g diced stewing beef

To cook:
1 tbsp olive oil

1 cup (240ml) boiling water

 ## IF MAKING AHEAD TO FREEZE

1 Put everything apart from the stewing beef into a large labelled freezer bag and mix together.

2 Put the diced beef into a separate freezer bag and slot inside the larger freezer bag, then seal and freeze flat.

 ### HOB

Remove the bags from the freezer and leave to fully defrost. Place a casserole dish on the hob on a high heat and add a tablespoon of olive oil. Add the beef and brown all over in batches. Once the beef is browned, add the rest of the ingredients. Pour over the boiling water, bring to the boil and stir, then pop the lid on and leave to cook on a low heat for 3 hours. Once it's tender, shred the beef with two forks.

SLOW COOKER

Remove the bags from the freezer and leave to fully defrost. Turn the slow cooker to the sauté setting. Add a tablespoon of olive oil and brown the beef all over in batches. Once the beef is browned, add the rest of the ingredients and mix. Pour over the boiling water, give it a good stir, then pop the lid on and cook for 4 hours on high, or 8 hours on low. Once it's tender, shred the beef with two forks.

PRESSURE COOKER

Remove the bags from the freezer and leave to fully defrost. Turn the pressure cooker to sauté. Add a tablespoon of olive oil and brown the beef all over in batches. Once the beef is browned, add the rest of the ingredients, stir well and pour over the boiling water. Seal the lid and cook for 30 minutes, then allow the steam to naturally release. Once it's tender, shred the beef with two forks.

 ## IF COOKING NOW

 ### HOB

Place a casserole dish on the hob on a high heat and add a tablespoon of olive oil. Add the beef and brown all over in batches. Once the beef is browned, add the rest of the ingredients, stir well and pour over the boiling water. Bring to the boil, then pop the lid on and leave to cook on a low heat for 3 hours. Once it's tender, shred the beef with two forks.

 ### SLOW COOKER

Turn the slow cooker to the sauté setting. Add a tablespoon of olive oil and brown the beef all over in batches. Once the beef is browned, add the rest of the ingredients, stir well, and pour over the boiling water. Give everything a good mix, then pop the lid on and cook for 4 hours on high, or 8 hours on low. Once it's tender, shred the beef with two forks.

 ### PRESSURE COOKER

Turn the pressure cooker to the sauté setting. Add a tablespoon of olive oil and brown the beef in batches. Once it is all browned, add the rest of the ingredients, stir well and pour over the boiling water. Seal the lid and cook for 30 minutes, then allow the steam to naturally release. Once it's tender, shred the beef with two forks.

TIP

Serve with pappardelle with lots of finely grated Parmesan.

CHEESY COD & PARSLEY PIE

This all-in-one fish pie is the ultimate grab-and-cook recipe. It takes 5 minutes to make and is the perfect weeknight meal to have in the freezer, ready to throw into the oven or microwave when you need it. It is cheesy, creamy and perfect for the whole family. For this recipe, I recommend using a glass dish with a plastic lid that can go straight from the freezer to the oven or microwave once the lid is removed.

Prep: 5 minutes | **Serves:** 4

320g skinless cod fillets, cut into small chunks

1 cup (140g) frozen peas

165g cream cheese

1 cup (240ml) double cream

⅔ cup (60g) grated Parmesan

a large handful of fresh parsley, finely chopped

salt and pepper

425g (about 1½ packs) ready-made mashed potato

❄ IF MAKING AHEAD TO FREEZE

1 Put the cod into a glass ovenproof dish and add the frozen peas, cream cheese, double cream, two-thirds of the grated Parmesan and two-thirds of the chopped parsley (reserving the rest of both to top the pie). Season with salt and pepper, and mix well.

2 Spread the ready-made mash over the top of the filling to cover it, then sprinkle over the remaining Parmesan and parsley to finish.

3 Put the lid on the dish and place it in the freezer.

🔲 OVEN

Preheat the oven to 200°C. Remove the lid of the dish and place the frozen fish pie in the oven for 1 hour, until bubbling and golden, covering with tin foil if it starts to burn.

🔲 MICROWAVE

Remove the lid and place the fish pie in the microwave for 8 minutes on the defrost setting, then 10–12 minutes on high power, until piping hot throughout and bubbling. Finish under a preheated grill for 6–7 minutes, until lovely and crisp.

IF COOKING NOW

Follow the method in the 'making ahead to freeze' section up until the end of step 2.

🔲 OVEN

Preheat the oven to 200°C. Cook the pie for 30 minutes, until bubbling and golden.

🔲 MICROWAVE

Remove the lid of the dish and place the fish pie in the microwave for approximately 10–12 minutes on high power, until the pie is piping hot throughout and bubbling. Finish under a preheated grill for 6–7 minutes, until lovely and crisp.

CREAMY SAUSAGE & CANNELLINI BEAN ONE-POT

I love an easy sausage one-pot, and this one ticks all the boxes. This recipe uses cannellini beans, but they can easily be swapped for chickpeas or butter beans if you prefer.

Prep: 5 minutes | **Serves:** 4

1 cup (115g) frozen diced onions

2 tsp frozen chopped garlic

2 cups (350g) frozen mixed chopped peppers

1 x 400g tin of cannellini beans, drained and rinsed

1 tsp smoked paprika

1 tsp dried oregano

scant 1 cup (200g) cream cheese

¾ cup (60g) grated Parmesan

1 chicken stock cube, crumbled

8 pork sausages

To cook:

1 tbsp olive oil

2 cups (500ml) boiling water

 ## IF MAKING AHEAD TO FREEZE

1 Put the onions, garlic, peppers, cannellini beans, smoked paprika, oregano, cream cheese, Parmesan and crumbled stock cube into a large freezer bag, mix together and freeze flat.

2 Keep the sausages in their packet, or put in a smaller freezer bag, and freeze alongside the bag of sauce.

 ### HOB

Remove from the freezer and leave to fully defrost. Put a tablespoon of olive oil into a large casserole dish and place on a medium heat. Add the pork sausages and brown them all over. Add the contents of the freezer bag, stir well, then pour over the boiling water. Bring to the boil, then reduce to a simmer and cook for 20 minutes.

 ### SLOW COOKER

Remove from the freezer and leave to fully defrost. Turn the slow cooker to the sauté setting and add a tablespoon of olive oil. Add the pork sausages and brown them all over. Add the contents of the freezer bag, stir well, then pour over the boiling water. Pop the lid on and cook for 3 hours on high, or 6 hours on low.

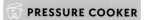 ### PRESSURE COOKER

Remove from the freezer and leave to fully defrost. Turn the pressure cooker to sauté and add a tablespoon of olive oil. Add the pork sausages and brown them all over. Once browned, add the contents of the freezer bag and pour over the boiling water. Give it a good mix, then seal the lid and cook for 9 minutes. Once cooked, allow the steam to quickly release.

 ## IF COOKING NOW

 ### HOB

Put a tablespoon of olive oil into a large casserole dish and place on a medium heat. Add the pork sausages and brown them all over, then add the rest of the ingredients. Pour over the boiling water and stir well. Bring to the boil, then reduce the heat to a simmer and cook for 20 minutes.

SLOW COOKER

Turn the slow cooker to the sauté setting and add a tablespoon of olive oil. Add the pork sausages and brown all over. Once browned, add the rest of the ingredients. Pour over the boiling water and stir well. Pop the lid on and cook for 3 hours on high, or 6 hours on low.

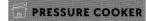 ### PRESSURE COOKER

Turn the pressure cooker to sauté and add a tablespoon of olive oil. Add the pork sausages and brown them all over, then add the rest of the ingredients. Pour over the boiling water, give it a good mix, then seal the lid and cook for 9 minutes. Once cooked, allow the steam to quickly release.

TIP

You can make this vegetarian with veggie sausages, a vegetarian Parmesan substitute and a vegetable stock cube.

JERK-SPICED HAKE PARCELS

These delicious hake parcels bring the flavours of Jamaica to you at home! Hake is similar to cod and haddock but is a cheaper and more sustainable alternative – why not give it a go?

Prep: 5 minutes | **Serves:** 4

4 tsp jerk seasoning paste

1 tsp runny honey

2 tsp frozen chopped ginger

2 tsp frozen chopped garlic

juice of 1 lime

1½ cups (260g) frozen mixed sliced peppers

1 x 210g tin of kidney beans, drained and rinsed

4 hake fillets (approx. 130g each)

a large handful of fresh coriander, roughly chopped

 ## IF MAKING AHEAD TO FREEZE

1   Put the jerk paste, honey, ginger, garlic and lime juice into a small bowl and mix well. Set this marinade aside.
2   Cut 4 squares of tin foil, each roughly 35 x 30cm.
3   Divide the sliced peppers and kidney beans between the tin foil squares and place a hake fillet on top of each one.
4   Spread the marinade over the fish, dividing it evenly between the parcels. Add a sprinkle of chopped coriander and fold the parcels up to seal.
5   Place the parcels in a labelled freezer bag and freeze flat.

 ### OVEN

Preheat the oven to 180°C. Place the frozen parcels on a baking tray and cook them for 30 minutes, until the hake is cooked through.

AIR FRYER

Preheat the air fryer to 180°C. Place the frozen parcels in the air fryer and cook them for 20–25 minutes, until the hake is cooked through.

 ## IF COOKING NOW

Follow the method in the 'making ahead to freeze' section up until the end of step 4.

 ### OVEN

Preheat the oven to 180°C. Place the parcels on a baking tray and cook them for 20–25 minutes, until the hake is cooked through.

AIR FRYER

Preheat the air fryer to 180°C. Place the parcels in the air fryer and cook them for 13–15 minutes, until the hake is cooked through.

 TIP
Serve with steamed basmati rice.

MINTED LAMB BURGERS

These burgers are super easy to make and they are a great thing to have in the freezer for a quick midweek meal or a weekend barbecue. This recipe makes 8 small burgers, and I like to serve 2 each.

Prep: 5 minutes | **Serves:** 4

500g lamb mince

1 red onion, finely diced

1 tsp frozen chopped garlic

1 tbsp dried mint

1 tsp salt

a good grind of black pepper

 IF MAKING AHEAD TO FREEZE

1 Put all the ingredients into a large bowl and mix together with your hands.

2 Tip the mix onto a work surface and divide in half. Split each half into 4 to give you 8 equal-sized pieces. Roll each piece into a ball, then press down to form a burger shape.

3 Open your large labelled freezer bag. Keeping the bag flat, put in the burgers, leaving space so they don't stick together. If stacking them on top of each other, add a layer of baking parchment to stop them sticking. Place flat in the freezer until fully frozen.

OVEN

Preheat the oven to 180°C. Put the frozen burgers on a grill tray lined with foil and cook for 25 minutes, turning over halfway through, until browned.

AIR FRYER

Preheat the oven to 180°C. Put the frozen burgers into the air fryer and cook for 16–17 minutes, turning over halfway through, until browned.

 IF COOKING NOW

Follow the method in the 'making ahead to freeze' section up until the end of step 2.

OVEN

Preheat the oven to 180°C. Place the burgers on a grill tray lined with foil and cook for 15 minutes, turning them over halfway through, until browned.

HOB

Place a non-stick frying pan on the hob on a medium heat. Put in the burgers and cook for 3–4 minutes on each side until browned and cooked through.

AIR FRYER

Preheat the air fryer to 180°C. Cook the burgers for 12 minutes, turning over halfway through, until browned.

TIP

Serve in pitta breads with tzatziki and salad.

SMOKED SAUSAGE GNOCCHI BAKE

This super easy one-pan bake is one of my favourite weeknight meals, and the kids love it! This recipe uses shop-bought cooked smoked sausage – you will find these in the cooked meats section of the supermarket.

Prep: 5 minutes | **Serves:** 4

500g fresh gnocchi

1 cup (115g) frozen diced onions

2 cups (500ml) passata

1 x 400g tin of chopped tomatoes

2 tsp frozen chopped garlic

1 tsp dried oregano

160g ready-to-eat cooked smoked sausage, sliced into chunks

1 cup (175g) frozen mixed sliced peppers

1 cup (140g) grated mozzarella

½ cup (70g) grated Cheddar

 IF MAKING AHEAD TO FREEZE

1 Put the gnocchi, onions, passata, chopped tomatoes, garlic, oregano, smoked sausage and peppers into a large freezer bag and mix.

2 Put all the grated cheese into a smaller freezer bag, and slot it inside the bigger freezer bag containing everything else. Freeze flat.

OVEN

Remove from the freezer and leave to fully defrost. Preheat the oven to 180°C. Pour the gnocchi mix into a medium-sized ovenproof dish and scatter over the grated cheese. Place in the oven for 30–40 minutes, until golden.

AIR FRYER

Remove from the freezer and leave to fully defrost. Preheat the air fryer to 175°C. Pour the gnocchi mixture into an air fryer-safe dish, reserving the cheese for later, and cook for 17–18 minutes, until bubbling. Remove and give the gnocchi a good mix, then scatter over the cheese and put back into the air fryer for 6–8 minutes, until golden.

IF COOKING NOW

Follow the method in the 'making ahead to freeze' section up until the end of step 1.

OVEN

Preheat the oven to 180°C. Pour the mix into a medium-sized ovenproof dish. Scatter over all the cheese and place in the oven for 30–40 minutes, until golden.

AIR FRYER

Preheat the air fryer to 175°C. Pour the gnocchi mix into an air fryer-safe dish, reserving the cheese for later, and cook for 17–18 minutes, until bubbling. Remove and give the gnocchi a good mix, then scatter over the cheese and put back into the air fryer for 6–8 minutes, until golden.

TIP

To make this vegetarian, you can use vegetarian smoked sausage.

ROMANO STUFFED PEPPERS

I love a good meat-free Monday and this recipe is just the thing for it – sweet peppers stuffed with fajita-spiced lentils and spinach, packed full of goodness and so delicious. I like to serve these with a drizzle of yoghurt and some fresh coriander. They work great as a barbecue side dish or an easy al fresco dinner!

Prep: 5 minutes | **Serves:** 4

2 x 400g tins of green lentils, drained and rinsed

2 tbsp fajita seasoning

1 red onion, finely diced

2 tsp frozen chopped garlic

2 tbsp tomato purée

2 tbsp olive oil

50g fresh spinach, finely chopped

salt and pepper

4 large romano peppers, cut in half lengthways, seeds removed

❄ IF MAKING AHEAD TO FREEZE

1 Put the lentils, fajita seasoning, red onion, frozen garlic, tomato purée, oil, spinach and a good grind of salt and pepper into a bowl and mix well.
2 Lay the 8 pepper halves on a board. Divide the lentil mixture evenly between them and press down to secure the mix.
3 Carefully put the stuffed peppers into a large labelled freezer bag in a single layer, stuffed side up. Place in the freezer and freeze flat.

OVEN

Preheat the oven to 180°C. Put the frozen stuffed peppers, stuffed side up, on a lined baking tray and cook for 25 minutes.

AIR FRYER

Preheat the air fryer to 180°C. Put the frozen stuffed peppers, stuffed side up, into the air fryer and cook for 13–14 minutes.

IF COOKING NOW

Follow the method in the 'making ahead to freeze' section up until the end of step 2.

OVEN

Preheat the oven to 180°C. Put the stuffed peppers, stuffed side up, on a lined baking tray and cook for 20 minutes.

AIR FRYER

Preheat the air fryer to 180°C. Put the stuffed peppers, stuffed side up, into the air fryer and cook for 12–13 minutes.

PIZZA PASTA SAUCE

This pasta sauce is a real kiddy crowd-pleaser – it takes no time at all on the hob, but you can choose a different cooking option to suit you. I always triple this recipe so I've got extra portions in the freezer.

Prep: 5 minutes | **Serves:** 4

1 cup (115g) frozen diced onions

2 tsp frozen chopped garlic

2 cups (500ml) passata

1 x 400g tin of chopped tomatoes

a large handful of fresh basil, roughly chopped

12 slices of pepperoni, cut into smaller slices

1 green pepper, deseeded and finely diced

½ cup (70g) frozen sweetcorn

1 tsp dried oregano

½ tsp caster sugar

salt and pepper

½ cup (70g) grated mozzarella

IF MAKING AHEAD TO FREEZE

1 Combine all the ingredients apart from the grated mozzarella in a large labelled freezer bag.

2 Put the grated mozzarella into a smaller bag, then seal and slot inside the larger bag. Freeze flat.

HOB

Put the frozen sauce into a large saucepan and gently defrost on a low heat, breaking it up with the back of a spoon as it defrosts. Once defrosted, bring to the boil, then reduce the heat and simmer for 20 minutes, stirring regularly. Once cooked, remove from the heat and stir in the grated mozzarella before serving.

SLOW COOKER

Put the frozen sauce into the slow cooker and turn it on. Pop the lid on, then cook for 3–4 hours on high or 6–7 hours on low, giving it a good stir halfway through. Once cooked, stir in the grated mozzarella before serving.

PRESSURE COOKER

Put the frozen sauce into the pressure cooker and cook on the sauté setting for 5–10 minutes, breaking it up with the back of a spoon until mostly defrosted. Place the lid on, seal, and cook on high pressure for 12 minutes. Quickly release the steam, then stir in the grated mozzarella before serving.

IF COOKING NOW

HOB

Put everything, except the grated mozzarella, into a large saucepan, mix and bring to the boil, then reduce to a simmer for 20 minutes, stirring regularly. Remove from the heat and stir in the grated mozzarella before serving.

SLOW COOKER

Put everything, except the grated mozzarella, into the slow cooker, stir, pop the lid on and cook for 3 hours on high, or 6 hours on low. Once cooked, stir in the grated mozzarella before serving.

PRESSURE COOKER

Put everything, except the grated mozzarella, into the pressure cooker and stir. Seal the lid and cook for 12 minutes on high pressure, then quickly release the steam and stir in the grated mozzarella before serving.

TIP

Serve with the pasta of your choice, with some garlic bread on the side. and garnish with fresh basil, if you like.

SPRING GREENS & COLEY PARCELS

I love an easy parcel recipe that can go straight into the oven from frozen. This recipe is lovely and fresh – it uses coley, but you can use any other white fish, such as haddock or cod.

Prep: 5 minutes | **Serves:** 4

2 cups (280g) frozen peas

4 spring onions, finely chopped

a handful of fresh dill, finely chopped

2 tsp frozen chopped garlic

zest and juice of 1 lemon

3 tbsp crème fraîche

salt and pepper

4 coley fillets (approx. 130g each)

olive oil, to drizzle

❄️ IF MAKING AHEAD TO FREEZE

1 Put the frozen peas, spring onions, dill, garlic, lemon zest and juice and crème fraîche into a bowl. Season well with salt and pepper, then mix to combine and set aside.

2 Cut 4 squares of tin foil, each roughly 35 x 30cm.

3 Divide the pea mixture between the tin foil squares, placing it in the centre of each square. Put the coley fillets on top, season with salt and pepper, and add a drizzle of olive oil. Carefully seal the parcels tightly.

4 Put the parcels into a large labelled freezer bag and freeze flat.

OVEN

Preheat the oven to 180°C. Place the frozen parcels on a baking tray and cook them for 30 minutes, until the fish is cooked through.

AIR FRYER

Preheat the air fryer to 180°C. Place the frozen parcels in the air fryer and cook for 20–25 minutes, until the fish is cooked through and tender.

🍲 IF COOKING NOW

Follow the method in the 'making ahead to freeze' section up until the end of step 3.

OVEN

Preheat the oven to 180°C. Place the parcels on a baking tray and cook them for 20–25 minutes, until the fish is cooked through.

AIR FRYER

Preheat the air fryer to 180°C. Place the parcels in the air fryer and cook for 13–15 minutes, until the fish is cooked through.

TIP

Serve with minted new potatoes.

SPINACH, PEA & MINT PASTA

This pasta sauce is lovely, fresh and zingy! Packed full of goodness and totally delicious. Simply put everything into a blender and blitz – it's as easy as that! This recipe shows you how to cook your pasta in the microwave, ready to top with the sauce – it works great, so give it a go!

Prep: 5 minutes | **Serves:** 4

1 cup (140g) frozen peas, defrosted

100g fresh spinach or 4 cubes of frozen spinach, defrosted

3 tsp frozen chopped garlic

a large handful of fresh mint

a large handful of fresh parsley

zest and juice of 1 lemon

4 tbsp olive oil

salt and pepper

 IF MAKING AHEAD TO FREEZE

1 Put everything into a blender, season with salt and pepper, and blitz until you have a smooth sauce.

2 Pour the sauce into a labelled freezer bag and freeze flat.

 MICROWAVE

Remove the sauce from the freezer, put it into a microwave-safe dish and defrost on the defrost setting. Once defrosted, set aside. Put 3 cups (300g) of penne pasta into a large, microwave-safe bowl, add ½ teaspoon of salt and cover with 6¾ cups (1.6 litres) of boiling water. Cook in the microwave on high power for 5 minutes, then remove, stir, and put back into the microwave for a further 5 minutes. Once cooked, scoop out a little cupful of the pasta water, then drain the pasta. Put the cooked pasta back into the bowl, and add the defrosted sauce and a splash of the pasta water. Mix and serve.

 HOB

Remove the sauce from the freezer. Put the frozen sauce into a large saucepan and leave to defrost slowly on a low heat, breaking it up with the back of a spoon. While the sauce is defrosting, get 3 cups (300g) of penne pasta on to cook in a saucepan of boiling water. Drain the pasta once cooked, reserving a little cupful of the pasta water. Add the cooked pasta to the sauce. Stir well on a low heat, add a splash of the pasta water to bring the dish together, then serve.

 IF COOKING NOW

Follow the method in the 'making ahead to freeze' section up until the end of step 1.

 MICROWAVE

Put 3 cups (300g) of penne pasta into a large, microwave-safe bowl, add ½ teaspoon of salt and cover with 6¾ cups (1.6 litres) of boiling water. Cook in the microwave on high power for 5 minutes, then remove, stir, and put back into the microwave for a further 5 minutes. Once cooked, scoop out a little cupful of the pasta water, then drain the pasta. Put the cooked pasta back into the bowl, and add the blended sauce and a splash of the pasta water. Mix and serve.

HOB

Get 3 cups (300g) of penne pasta on to cook in a saucepan of boiling water. Drain the pasta once cooked, reserving a little cupful of the pasta water. Put the cooked pasta back into the saucepan and pour over the blended sauce. Stir well on a low heat, add a splash of the pasta water to bring the dish together, then serve.

TIP

Serve with garlic bread and lots of freshly grated Parmesan (or a vegetarian or vegan alternative if necessary).

BAKED HONEY & MUSTARD PORK CHOPS

Pork chops make a great midweek dinner – they are inexpensive and help to add variety to your weekly meal plan. This recipe is so quick and easy you can't go wrong.

Prep: 5 minutes | **Serves:** 4

1 tbsp wholegrain mustard

2 tbsp Dijon mustard

3 tbsp runny honey

1 tsp soy sauce

2 tsp frozen chopped garlic

4 bone-in pork chops

 IF MAKING AHEAD TO FREEZE

1 Put both mustards, the honey, soy sauce and garlic into a small bowl and mix to combine.

2 Put the pork chops into a large labelled freezer bag and pour over the sauce. Mix, then seal and freeze flat.

 OVEN

Remove from the freezer and leave to fully defrost. Preheat the oven to 180°C. Pour the chops and sauce into a roasting tin. Cook for 20 minutes, spooning the juices over the chops halfway through.

 AIR FRYER

Remove from the freezer and leave to fully defrost. Preheat the air fryer to 180°C. Put the pork chops and sauce into an air fryer-safe dish and cook for 15–16 minutes, flipping them over and spooning the juices over the chops halfway through.

 IF COOKING NOW

Follow the method in the 'making ahead to freeze' section up until the end of step 1.

 OVEN

Preheat the oven to 180°C. Put the pork chops into a roasting tin and pour over the sauce. Cook for 20 minutes, spooning the juices over the chops halfway through.

 AIR FRYER

Preheat the air fryer to 180°C. Put the pork chops into an air fryer-safe dish and pour over the sauce. Cook for 15–16 minutes, flipping them over and spooning the juices over the chops halfway through.

TIP
Serve with mashed potatoes and seasonal greens!

MEDITERRANEAN GNOCCHI PESTO BAKE

This gnocchi bake is a brilliant all-in-one meal – no need to add a side of vegetables, as it is already packed with them. I love using gnocchi as an alternative to pasta, and it helps to add variety to my weekly meal plan.

Prep: 5 minutes | **Serves:** 4

500g fresh gnocchi

1 red onion, diced into thick chunks

1 medium aubergine, diced into 2cm chunks

300g cherry tomatoes

1 small courgette, cut into 2cm chunks

3 tbsp olive oil

1 tbsp dried oregano

4 heaped tbsp pesto

salt and pepper

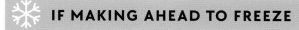

❄ IF MAKING AHEAD TO FREEZE

1 Put everything into a large labelled freezer bag, season with salt and pepper, mix well and freeze flat.

OVEN

Remove from the freezer and leave to fully defrost. Preheat the oven to 180°C. Once defrosted, put everything into a medium-sized, ovenproof dish and cook for 35 minutes, giving it a good stir halfway through.

AIR FRYER

Remove from the freezer and leave to fully defrost. Preheat the air fryer to 180°C. Once defrosted, pour it all into an air fryer-safe dish and cook for 20 minutes, giving everything a good shake halfway through.

IF COOKING NOW

OVEN

Preheat the oven to 180°C. Put all the ingredients into a medium-sized, ovenproof dish, season with salt and pepper and give it a good mix. Place in the oven for 35 minutes, giving it a stir halfway through.

AIR FRYER

Preheat the air fryer to 180°C. Put everything into an air fryer-safe dish, season with salt and pepper and give it a good mix. Place in the air fryer and cook for 20 minutes, giving everything a shake halfway through.

TIP

To make this vegan, use a plant-based pesto and gnocchi.

PIZZA-STUFFED CHICKEN BREASTS

If you are craving pizza, these stuffed chicken breasts will hit the spot, and these are great for the kids! Filled with pepperoni, mozzarella and basil, what's not to love? This recipe uses shop-bought pizza sauce, but you can make your own by following the Pizza Pasta Sauce recipe on page 114.

Prep: 5–10 minutes | **Serves:** 4

4 skinless and boneless chicken breasts

4 tbsp shop-bought pizza sauce

1 x 240g ball of mozzarella, drained and cut into 8 slices

12 slices of pepperoni

a handful of fresh basil leaves

2 tsp paprika

2 tbsp olive oil

 IF MAKING AHEAD TO FREEZE

1 Place the chicken breasts on a chopping board and cut down the side of each one to create a pocket, making sure you don't cut all the way through the breast.
2 Working with one chicken breast at a time, open the pocket and add 1 tablespoon of pizza sauce, 2 slices of mozzarella, 3 slices of pepperoni and a few basil leaves. Fold the pocket over to enclose the filling. Repeat with the rest of the chicken breasts.
3 Put the paprika and olive oil into a shallow bowl and stir, then brush the paprika oil over each chicken breast.
4 Put the stuffed chicken breasts into a large labelled freezer bag and freeze flat.

 OVEN

Remove from the freezer and leave to fully defrost. Preheat the oven to 180°C. Place the chicken breasts on a lined baking tray and cook for 25–30 minutes, until the chicken is cooked through.

 AIR FRYER

Remove from the freezer and leave to fully defrost. Preheat the air fryer to 180°C. Place the stuffed chicken breasts in the air fryer and cook for 20 minutes, until the chicken is cooked through.

 IF COOKING NOW

Follow the method in the 'making ahead to freeze' section up until the end of step 3.

OVEN

Preheat the oven to 180°C. Place the stuffed chicken breasts on a lined baking tray and cook for 25–30 minutes, until the chicken is cooked through.

AIR FRYER

Preheat the air fryer to 180°C. Place the stuffed chicken breasts in the air fryer and cook for 20 minutes, until the chicken is cooked through.

TIP
Serve with chips and a side salad.

ROMESCO PASTA

Save cooking from scratch every single night – just make this fab pasta sauce, triple the recipe and you will have three easy pasta nights already sorted and in the freezer for busy weeks ahead. This recipe shows you how to cook pasta in the microwave, ready to top with your sauce. It works great – why not give it a go!

Prep: 5 minutes | **Serves:** 4

1 x 350g jar of roasted red peppers, drained

8 sun-dried tomatoes in oil, drained, plus 2 tbsp of their oil

2 tsp frozen chopped garlic

1 tsp smoked paprika

½ tsp chilli flakes

¼ cup (30g) ground almonds

 ## IF MAKING AHEAD TO FREEZE

1 Put all the ingredients into a blender and blend until smooth.

2 Put the sauce into a labelled freezer bag and freeze flat.

 ### MICROWAVE

Remove the sauce from the freezer, put it into a microwave-safe dish, and defrost on the defrost setting. Once defrosted, set aside. Put 3 cups (300g) of dried penne pasta into a large, microwave-safe bowl, add ½ teaspoon of salt and cover with 6¾ cups (1.6 litres) of boiling water. Cook in the microwave on high power for 5 minutes, then remove, stir, and put back into the microwave for a further 5 minutes. Once cooked, scoop out a little cupful of the pasta water, then drain the pasta. Put the cooked pasta back into the bowl, add the defrosted sauce and a little splash of the pasta water. Mix and serve.

HOB

Remove the sauce from the freezer. Put the frozen sauce into a large saucepan and leave to defrost slowly on a low heat, breaking it up with the back of a spoon. While the sauce is defrosting, get 3 cups (300g) of dried penne pasta on to cook in a saucepan of boiling water. Drain the pasta once cooked, reserving a little cupful of the pasta water. Add the cooked pasta to the sauce. Stir well on a low heat and add a splash of the pasta water to bring the dish together, then serve.

 ## IF COOKING NOW

Follow the 'making ahead to freeze' section up until the end of step 1.

 ### MICROWAVE

Put 3 cups (300g) of dried penne pasta into a large microwave-safe bowl, add ½ teaspoon of salt and cover with 6¾ cups (1.6 litres) of boiling water. Cook in the microwave on high power for 5 minutes, then remove, stir, and put back into the microwave for a further 5 minutes. Once cooked, scoop out a little cupful of the pasta water, then drain the pasta. Put the cooked pasta back into the bowl, add the blended sauce and a little splash of the pasta water. Mix and serve.

 ### HOB

Get 3 cups (300g) of dried penne pasta on to cook in a saucepan of boiling water. Drain the pasta once cooked, reserving a little cupful of the pasta water. Add the cooked pasta back to the saucepan and pour over the blended sauce. Stir well on a low heat and add a splash of the pasta water to bring the dish together, then serve.

TIP

Serve with garlic bread and lots of freshly grated Parmesan (or a vegetarian or vegan alternative if necessary).

CAJUN-SPICED SWEET POTATO CAKES

These crunchy potato cakes with Cajun spices are vibrant and delicious, a wonderful midweek meal.

Prep: 10 minutes | **Serves:** 4

1 x 400g pack of ready-made sweet potato mash

½ cup (70g) grated mozzarella

3 tsp Cajun seasoning

1 x 198g tin of sweetcorn, drained

1 cup (175g) frozen mixed sliced peppers

2 tbsp plain flour

salt and pepper

2 eggs, beaten

1½ cups (66g) panko breadcrumbs

To cook:
olive oil, to drizzle

 IF MAKING AHEAD TO FREEZE

1 Put the sweet potato mash, mozzarella, Cajun seasoning, sweetcorn, sliced peppers and plain flour into a mixing bowl and season well. Mix everything together.

2 Tip the mix out onto a work surface. Using your hands, divide the mix into 8 equal portions, then form each into a ball. Once you have 8 balls, lightly press each down to make a thick patty.

3 Set two shallow bowls on the work surface. Add the beaten eggs to one and the breadcrumbs to the other.

4 Take a patty and coat it in the beaten egg, then in the breadcrumbs. Repeat with the rest of the patties.

5 Open a large labelled freezer bag. Keeping it flat, put in the potato cakes, leaving space so they don't stick together. If stacking on top of each other, add a layer of baking parchment to stop them sticking. Place flat in the freezer until fully frozen.

OVEN

Preheat the oven to 190°C. Put the frozen potato cakes on a lined baking tray, drizzle with a little oil, and place in the oven for 30–40 minutes, until golden.

AIR FRYER

Preheat the air fryer to 190°C. Drizzle the frozen potato cakes with a little oil, then place in the air fryer and cook for 17–18 minutes, flipping halfway through, until golden.

IF COOKING NOW

Follow the method in the 'making ahead to freeze' section up until the end of step 4.

TIP
Serve with a big leafy salad and some fresh crusty bread.

OVEN

Preheat the oven to 190°C. Put the potato cakes on a lined baking tray, drizzle with a little oil, and place in the oven for 25–30 minutes, until golden.

AIR FRYER

Preheat the air fryer to 190°C. Drizzle the potato cakes with a little oil, then place in the air fryer and cook for 15 minutes, flipping halfway through, until golden.

CRUNCHY TOMATO, COD & PEA PARCELS

These super easy kiddy-friendly cod parcels are a saving grace to have in the freezer. They are so easy to make using sun-dried tomato pesto, and there's no need to worry about a vegetable side as you have your peas included.

Prep: 5 minutes | **Serves:** 4

2 cups (280g) frozen peas

4 cod fillets (approx. 160g each)

4 tbsp sun-dried tomato pesto

8 tbsp panko breadcrumbs

⅓ cup (47g) grated Cheddar

 IF MAKING AHEAD TO FREEZE

1 Cut 4 squares of tin foil, each roughly 35 x 30cm.
2 Divide the frozen peas between the tin foil squares, placing them in a pile in the centre of each one.
3 Place the cod fillets on top of the peas and spread each one with 1 tablespoon of pesto.

4 Mix the breadcrumbs and grated cheese in a small bowl, and distribute this breadcrumb mixture on top of the cod fillets – the pesto should help the breadcrumbs to stick. Wrap each parcel up carefully.
5 Put the wrapped parcels into a large labelled freezer bag and freeze flat.

 OVEN

Preheat the oven to 180°C. Place the frozen parcels on a baking tray, open them slightly at the top, and put in the oven for 30 minutes, until the cod is cooked through.

 AIR FRYER

Preheat the air fryer to 180°C. Place the frozen parcels in the air fryer and cook for 20–25 minutes. Open the parcels slightly at the top 5 minutes before the end of the cooking time, for a lovely crunchy top.

 IF COOKING NOW

Follow the method in the 'making ahead to freeze' section up until the end of step 4.

 OVEN

Preheat the oven to 180°C. Place the parcels on a baking tray, open them up slightly at the top, and cook for 20–25 minutes, until the cod is cooked through.

 AIR FRYER

Preheat the air fryer to 180°C. Place the parcels in the air fryer and cook for 13–15 minutes. Open them up slightly 5 minutes before the end of the cooking time, to get a lovely crunchy top.

TIP
Serve with crispy potato wedges or baked potatoes, and garnish with fresh dill, if you like.

BEEF OLIVES

Beef olives are a traditional Scottish recipe and a real comfort food – spiced sausage meat encased in thinly cut beef. A super quick midweek meal!

Prep: 5–10 minutes | **Serves:** 4

200g sausage meat

2 tsp dried sage

½ cup (58g) frozen diced onions

1 tbsp breadcrumbs

4 thinly cut beef steaks

To cook:
olive oil, to drizzle

 IF MAKING AHEAD TO FREEZE

1 Put the sausage meat, dried sage, diced onions and breadcrumbs into a large mixing bowl and mix together really well.
2 Lay the 4 beef steaks on a board in front of you. Place a quarter of the meat mix in a sausage shape down the centre of each beef steak. Roll up the beef steaks to enclose the filling and insert 2–3 cocktail sticks along the seal of each to keep the steak and filling secure.
3 Put the beef olives carefully into a large labelled freezer bag and freeze.

 OVEN

Remove from the freezer and leave to fully defrost. Preheat the oven to 200°C. Put the beef olives on a baking tray and drizzle with a little olive oil. Cook for 18–20 minutes.

AIR FRYER

Remove from the freezer and leave to fully defrost. Preheat the air fryer to 180°C. Place the beef olives in the air fryer and cook for 13–14 minutes, flipping them over halfway through.

 IF COOKING NOW

Follow the method in the 'making ahead to freeze' section up until the end of step 2.

 OVEN

Preheat the oven to 200°C. Put the beef olives on a baking tray and drizzle with a little olive oil. Cook for 18–20 minutes.

AIR FRYER

Preheat the air fryer to 180°C. Place the beef olives in the air fryer and cook for 13–14 minutes, flipping them over halfway through.

TIP

Serve with instant gravy, mash and seasonal veggies!

1 BARBECUE SPARE RIBS

2 BUTTERMILK CHICKEN BURGERS

3 ONION BHAJIS

4 LAMB JALFREZI MEATBALLS & CURRIED TOMATO SAUCE

5 STROMBOLI

6 VEGETABLE SPRING ROLLS

7 COCONUT-CRUSTED KING PRAWNS

8 SATAY CHICKEN CURRY

9 SESAME PRAWN TOASTS

10 SOY CHILLI BEEF & PEPPERS

11 TEX MEX BURGER

12 SLOW-COOKED CHIPOTLE CHICKEN & BLACK BEANS

13 PORK CARNITAS

14 HONEY SESAME CHICKEN

15 CURRYWURST

FAKEAWAYS

BARBECUE SPARE RIBS

The ultimate fakeaway! Spare ribs are a takeaway classic, and this recipe shows you how to make them at home for a fraction of the price. And they are even more delicious, in my opinion! These ribs are best finished under the grill, which isn't essential, but it does give the perfect sticky and crunchy coating.

Prep: 5 minutes | **Serves:** 4

½ cup (100g) light brown sugar

2 tsp garlic powder

2 tsp onion powder

2 tsp smoked paprika

1 tsp salt

1 cup (240ml) barbecue sauce

2 tbsp Worcestershire sauce

3 tbsp tomato ketchup

1.4kg pork ribs

To cook:
½ cup (120ml) boiling water

 ❄ **IF MAKING AHEAD TO FREEZE**

1 Put all the ingredients apart from the ribs into a large bowl. Mix everything together, then add the ribs and coat in the sauce.

2 Put everything into a large labelled freezer bag and freeze flat.

OVEN

Remove from the freezer and leave to fully defrost. Preheat the oven to 160°C. Put the ribs into a large, deep-sided roasting tin and pour over the boiling water. Cover well with tin foil and place in the oven for 2 hours. After 2 hours, remove the foil, turn the grill to high, and cook for a further 6–7 minutes to allow the ribs to crisp up.

SLOW COOKER

Remove from the freezer and leave to fully defrost. Put the ribs into the slow cooker and cover with the boiling water. Pop the lid on and cook for 5 hours on high, or 9 hours on low. Transfer the ribs to a baking tray and cook under a hot grill for 6–7 minutes to crisp them up.

 IF COOKING NOW

Follow the method in the 'making ahead to freeze' section up until the end of step 1.

OVEN

Preheat the oven to 160°C. Put the ribs into a large, deep-sided roasting tin and pour over the boiling water. Cover well with tin foil and place in the oven for 2 hours. After 2 hours, remove the foil, turn the grill to high, and cook for a further 6–7 minutes to allow the ribs to crisp up.

SLOW COOKER

Put the ribs into the slow cooker and cover with the boiling water. Pop the lid on and cook for 5 hours on high, or 9 hours on low. Transfer the ribs to a baking tray and cook under a hot grill for 6–7 minutes to crisp them up.

TIP
Serve with chips, coleslaw and corn on the cob!

BUTTERMILK CHICKEN BURGERS

These are so delicious and a brilliant fakeaway treat! The buttermilk makes the chicken extra juicy, and the flour coating gives a lovely crunch. You will find buttermilk next to the yoghurt and cream in the supermarket.

Prep: 10 minutes | **Serves:** 4

4 skinless and boneless chicken breasts

1¼ cups (300ml) buttermilk

1 cup (110g) plain flour

1 tsp smoked paprika

1 tsp garlic powder

1 tsp dried oregano

1 tsp salt

To cook:
vegetable oil, to drizzle

 IF MAKING AHEAD TO FREEZE

1 Place the chicken breasts between two layers of cling film. Using a rolling pin, bash the chicken flat until it is 2cm thick all over.

2 Place the chicken breasts in a bowl and pour over the buttermilk, coating all the chicken well. Cover and place in the fridge for 1 hour, to allow the chicken to tenderise.

3 Put the flour into a bowl with the smoked paprika, garlic powder, oregano and salt and mix to combine.

4 Remove the chicken breasts from the buttermilk one by one and gently shake, discarding any excess buttermilk, then place in the flour mix. Coat each chicken breast thoroughly in the flour and shake off any excess.

5 Open your large labelled freezer bag. Keeping the bag flat, put the chicken burgers inside, leaving space so they don't stick together. If stacking on top of each other, add a layer of baking parchment to stop them sticking. Place flat in the freezer until fully frozen.

 OVEN

Preheat the oven to 180°C. Place the frozen chicken burgers on a lined baking tray and drizzle with vegetable oil, then place in the oven for 30–35 minutes, until golden and cooked through.

AIR FRYER

Preheat the air fryer to 180°C. Drizzle the frozen chicken burgers with vegetable oil, place in the air fryer and cook for 25–30 minutes, flipping them over halfway, until golden and cooked through.

 IF COOKING NOW

Follow the method in the 'making ahead to freeze' section up until the end of step 4.

 OVEN

Preheat the oven to 180°C. Place the chicken burgers on a lined baking tray and drizzle with vegetable oil. Place into the oven for 25 minutes, until golden and cooked through.

AIR FRYER

Preheat the air fryer to 180°C. Drizzle the chicken burgers with vegetable oil, place in the air fryer and cook for 20–22 minutes, flipping them over halfway, until golden and cooked through.

TIP

Serve in brioche buns, with lettuce and mayo or whatever toppings you fancy, plus chips on the side.

ONION BHAJIS

Bhajis are a national favourite, and they are surprisingly easy to make at home! I love to serve these as a starter when I'm having an Indian-themed night, or alongside the Lamb Jalfrezi Meatballs on page 142 for a delicious side.

Prep: 10 minutes | **Makes:** 8

2 red onions, halved and finely sliced

30g fresh coriander, chopped

2 tsp frozen chopped ginger

2 tsp frozen chopped garlic

½ tsp chilli powder

2 tsp ground coriander

2 tsp ground cumin

1 tsp salt

1 cup (110g) gram flour

¼ cup plus 2 tablespoons (80ml) cold water

To cook:
vegetable oil, to drizzle

 IF MAKING AHEAD TO FREEZE

1 Put the red onions, fresh coriander, ginger, garlic, chilli powder, ground coriander, cumin, salt and gram flour into a mixing bowl. Mix well, then add the cold water and mix again until you have a thick batter that holds together.

2 Take a tablespoon of the batter and roll into a ball. Repeat to make 8 bhajis, placing on a lined baking tray as you go.

3 Place the baking tray in the freezer and flash freeze for 1 hour, then put the bhajis into a labelled freezer bag.

 OVEN

Preheat the oven to 190°C. Place the frozen bhajis on a lined baking tray, drizzle with vegetable oil and cook for 30 minutes, until golden.

 AIR FRYER

Preheat the air fryer to 180°C. Drizzle the frozen bhajis with vegetable oil and cook for 16–17 minutes, turning them over halfway through, until golden.

 IF COOKING NOW

Follow the method in the 'making ahead to freeze' section up until the end of step 2.

OVEN

Preheat the oven to 200°C. Drizzle the bhajis with vegetable oil and cook for 20–25 minutes, until golden.

HOB

Fill a pot 5cm deep with vegetable oil and place on a medium-high heat. Test if it's hot enough by dropping in a bit of bread – if it floats and starts to go golden, it's ready. Deep-fry the bhajis in batches for 3–4 minutes, until golden, then remove and place on kitchen paper.

AIR FRYER

Preheat the air fryer to 180°C. Drizzle the bhajis with vegetable oil and cook for 15 minutes, turning them over halfway through, until golden.

TIP
Serve with mango chutney and yoghurt (use plant-based if cooking for vegans) with chopped mint.

LAMB JALFREZI MEATBALLS & CURRIED TOMATO SAUCE

All the flavours of a classic jalfrezi curry but inside a lamb meatball, with a delicious rich curried sauce.

Prep: 10–15 minutes | **Serves:** 4

For the meatballs:
500g lamb mince

2 tbsp jalfrezi curry paste

2 tsp frozen chopped garlic

2 tsp frozen chopped ginger

a large handful of fresh coriander, finely chopped

1 tsp salt

a good grind of pepper

For the sauce:
2 x 400g tins of chopped tomatoes

1 cup (115g) frozen diced onions

1 cup (175g) frozen mixed sliced peppers

1 tbsp jalfrezi curry paste

To cook:
olive oil

TIP
Serve with rice, poppadoms and mango chutney.

IF MAKING AHEAD TO FREEZE

1 Put all the meatball ingredients into a bowl and mix with your hands. Tip onto a work surface and bring everything together. Split the mix in half and then into quarters. Divide each quarter into 4 and roll each piece into a ball.

2 Put the meatballs into a large labelled freezer bag.

3 Put all the sauce ingredients into a separate freezer bag and seal, then place inside the bag of meatballs, seal and freeze flat.

HOB

Remove from the freezer and leave to fully defrost. Place a large, deep-sided frying pan on a medium heat and add a splash of olive oil. Brown the meatballs all over, then pour in the bag of sauce. Bring to the boil, then reduce to a simmer and cook for 20 minutes.

SLOW COOKER

Remove from the freezer and leave to fully defrost. Turn the slow cooker on to the sauté setting and add a splash of oil. Add the meatballs and brown them all over, then pour in the bag of sauce. Mix well, put the lid on and cook for 3–4 hours on high, or 6–7 hours on low.

IF COOKING NOW

Follow the method in the 'make ahead to freeze' section up until the end of step 1.

HOB

Place a large, deep-sided frying pan on a medium heat and add a splash of olive oil. Brown the meatballs all over, then add the sauce ingredients. Bring to the boil, then reduce to a simmer and cook for 20 minutes.

SLOW COOKER

Turn the slow cooker on to the sauté setting and add a splash of olive oil. Add the meatballs and brown them all over, then add all the sauce ingredients. Mix well, put the lid on and cook for 3–4 hours on high, or 6–7 hours on low.

STROMBOLI

If you've never had stromboli before, I promise it will become your new favourite Friday night fakeaway. Stromboli is basically a rolled-up pizza. Feel free to change the fillings to whatever you fancy!

Prep: 10–15 minutes | **Serves:** 4

1 roll of ready-made pizza dough (400g)

5 tbsp shop-bought pizza sauce

a large handful of grated Cheddar

1 cup (140g) grated mozzarella

8 large slices of salami

½ cup (80g) frozen sweetcorn

2 large mushrooms, finely chopped

6 fresh basil leaves

1 egg, beaten

1 tsp dried oregano

 **IF MAKING AHEAD TO FREEZE**

1   Unroll the pizza dough, keeping it on its paper, with the long side nearest you. Spread over the pizza sauce, leaving a 2.5cm border on the length furthest from you.
2   Sprinkle over the Cheddar and mozzarella, then lay over the salami slices and sprinkle over the sweetcorn, mushrooms and basil leaves.
3   Brush some of the beaten egg on the empty border on the dough.
4   Roll it up like a burrito. Tuck the sides in, then begin rolling to create a log.
5   Brush the stromboli with beaten egg and sprinkle over the dried oregano.
6   Fold up the sides of the paper, then wrap well with cling film. Place in a large labelled freezer bag and freeze flat.

OVEN

Preheat the oven to 190°C. Place the frozen stromboli, cling film removed but still on its paper, on a baking tray and cook for 30–35 minutes.

AIR FRYER

Preheat the air fryer to 180°C. Place the frozen stromboli (cling film removed but still in its paper) on a sheet of baking parchment and cook for 18 minutes, then flip over, peel off the pizza dough paper, and cook for a further 5 minutes.

 IF COOKING NOW

Follow the method in the 'making ahead to freeze' section up until the end of step 5.

OVEN

Preheat the oven to 190°C. Place the stromboli, still on its paper, on a baking tray and cook for 25 minutes.

AIR FRYER

Preheat the air fryer to 180°C. Place the stromboli on a sheet of baking parchment and cook for 14 minutes, then flip it over, peel off the pizza dough paper, and cook for a further 4–6 minutes.

TIP
Serve with a big green salad.

VEGETABLE SPRING ROLLS

These are crunchy, packed full of flavour, and just the recipe for your next Friday night fakeaway. You will find spring roll wrappers in the world food aisle of the supermarket or in an Asian supermarket. Why not stir-fry any leftover beansprouts with some noodles and serve as a side dish?

Prep: 10 minutes | **Makes:** 12

5 medium mushrooms, very finely diced

1 medium carrot, peeled and coarsely grated

100g beansprouts

1 red chilli, deseeded and finely diced

2 spring onions, finely sliced

3 tsp frozen chopped garlic

3 tsp frozen chopped ginger

a large handful of fresh coriander, finely chopped

1 tbsp soy sauce

1 tbsp sesame oil

1 pack of large spring roll wrappers

To cook:
2 tbsp vegetable oil

 IF MAKING AHEAD TO FREEZE

1 Put all the ingredients apart from the spring roll wrappers into a large bowl and mix well.
2 Place a spring roll wrapper on the counter in front of you and turn it so it looks like a diamond. Add 1 heaped tablespoon of the mix, 2.5cm from the corner closest to you. Flip the bottom corner over the filling and then roll over, folding in the sides as you go, until you have a lovely neat roll. Repeat to make the rest of the 12 spring rolls.
3 Put them into a large labelled freezer bag and freeze flat.

 OVEN

Preheat the oven to 200°C. Put the frozen spring rolls on a baking tray and drizzle with the vegetable oil. Place in the oven and cook for 25 minutes, until golden.

AIR FRYER

Preheat the air fryer to 200°C. Drizzle the frozen spring rolls with the vegetable oil and cook for 15–18 minutes, giving them a shake halfway through, until golden.

 IF COOKING NOW

Follow the method in the 'making ahead to freeze' section up until the end of step 2.

 OVEN

Preheat the oven to 200°C. Put the spring rolls on a baking tray and drizzle with the vegetable oil. Place in the oven and cook for 20 minutes, until golden.

AIR FRYER

Preheat the air fryer to 200°C. Drizzle the spring rolls with the vegetable oil and cook for 9–11 minutes, giving them a shake halfway through, until golden.

TIP
Serve with sweet chilli sauce or sweet and sour sauce.

COCONUT-CRUSTED KING PRAWNS

These crunchy coated prawns are just divine – they are so good dunked in sweet chilli sauce. I love to serve them with the Vegetable Spring Rolls on page 147 as a lovely starter or side to a Chinese family feast.

Prep: 10 minutes | **Serves:** 4

¾ cup (83g) plain flour

2 eggs, beaten

zest of 1 lime

1 cup (50g) panko breadcrumbs

3 tbsp desiccated coconut

½ tsp salt

330g raw king prawns, peeled

To cook:
2 tbsp vegetable oil

 IF MAKING AHEAD TO FREEZE

1 Place 3 shallow bowls on the work surface. Put the flour into the first bowl, the eggs into the second bowl, and in the third bowl, mix the lime zest, panko breadcrumbs, desiccated coconut and salt.

2 One at a time, dip each prawn into the flour, then the egg, then the breadcrumbs, making sure to coat well at each stage.

3 Put the prawns on a lined tray and flash freeze for 1 hour, then put them into a large labelled freezer bag.

OVEN

Preheat the oven to 200°C. Place the frozen prawns on a lined baking tray and drizzle with the vegetable oil. Bake for 11–12 minutes, until crisp.

AIR FRYER

Preheat the air fryer to 200°C. Drizzle the frozen prawns with the vegetable oil, place in the air fryer and cook for 7–8 minutes, giving it a shake halfway through.

 IF COOKING NOW

Follow the method in the 'making ahead to freeze' section up until the end of step 2.

OVEN

Preheat the oven to 200°C. Place the prawns on a lined baking tray and drizzle with the vegetable oil. Bake for 8–10 minutes, until crisp.

AIR FRYER

Preheat the air fryer to 200°C. Drizzle the prawns with the vegetable oil, place in the air fryer and cook for 5–6 minutes, giving it a shake halfway through.

TIP
Serve with lots of sweet chilli sauce and lime wedges for squeezing over.

SATAY CHICKEN CURRY

This is one of my favourite curries! The mild coconut peanut sauce is so delicious, and it's the perfect balance of sweet and savoury. If you're a peanut lover, this one's for you!

Prep: 5 minutes | **Serves:** 4

650g skinless and boneless chicken thighs

2 cups (350g) frozen mixed sliced peppers

3 tsp frozen chopped garlic

3 tsp frozen chopped ginger

1 onion, finely sliced

3 tbsp crunchy peanut butter

1 tbsp mild curry powder

1 tbsp runny honey

2 tbsp soy sauce

juice of 1 lime

1 tbsp frozen chopped coriander

1 chicken stock cube, crumbled

1 x 400ml tin of coconut milk

 IF MAKING AHEAD TO FREEZE

Put all the ingredients into a large labelled freezer bag, mix well, then freeze flat.

HOB

Remove from the freezer and leave to fully defrost, then pour into a large saucepan or casserole dish. Bring to the boil, then reduce to a simmer. Pop the lid on the pan and cook for 45–50 minutes, stirring often. Once cooked, shred the chicken using two forks.

SLOW COOKER

Remove from the freezer and leave to fully defrost, then pour into the slow cooker. Pop the lid on and cook for 4 hours on high, or 8 hours on low. Once cooked, shred the chicken using two forks.

PRESSURE COOKER

Remove from the freezer and leave to fully defrost, then pour into the pressure cooker. Seal the lid and cook for 16 minutes on high pressure, then allow it to naturally release. Once cooked, shred the chicken using two forks.

 IF COOKING NOW

HOB

Put all the ingredients into a large saucepan or casserole dish and mix. Bring to the boil, then reduce to a simmer, pop the lid on and cook for 45–50 minutes, stirring often. Once cooked, shred the chicken using two forks.

SLOW COOKER

Put all the ingredients into the slow cooker and mix. Pop the lid on and cook for 4 hours on high, or 8 hours on low. Once cooked, shred the chicken using two forks.

PRESSURE COOKER

Put all the ingredients into the pressure cooker and mix. Seal the lid and cook for 16 minutes on high pressure, then allow it to naturally release. Once cooked, shred the chicken using two forks.

TIP

Serve with fluffy rice, fresh coriander and a squeeze of lime.

SESAME PRAWN TOASTS

Prawn toast is a Chinese takeaway staple and it's surprisingly easy to make at home! I love to serve these as a side or a starter if I'm having a Chinese night at home – they go really well with the Soy Chilli Beef & Peppers on page 154!

Prep: 10 minutes | **Serves:** 4 (makes 16 triangles)

200g raw prawns, peeled

2 tsp frozen chopped garlic

3 tsp frozen chopped ginger

3 spring onions, roughly chopped

1 tsp caster sugar

1 tbsp soy sauce

1 egg white

4 thick slices of white bread

1 tbsp sesame oil

½ cup (60g) sesame seeds

To cook:
vegetable oil

 IF MAKING AHEAD TO FREEZE

1 Put the prawns into a food processor with the garlic, ginger, spring onions, sugar, soy sauce and egg white and blitz until smooth.
2 Lay out the 4 slices of bread on a work surface. Brush each slice with a little sesame oil, then spread the prawn mix over the 4 slices.
3 Put the sesame seeds on a flat plate and press the bread, prawn side down, into the seeds. Repeat with the other slices. Cut each slice into 4 triangles.
4 Open a large labelled freezer bag. Keeping the bag flat, put in the triangles, prawn side up, leaving space so they don't stick together. If stacking them on top of each other, add a layer of baking parchment to stop them sticking. Place flat in the freezer until fully frozen.

 HOB

Heat a good glug of vegetable oil in a non-stick frying pan on a medium heat. Once hot, add the frozen prawn toasts, prawn side down, and cook in batches for 3–4 minutes on each side, until golden.

AIR FRYER

Preheat the air fryer to 180°C. Drizzle the frozen prawn toasts with a little vegetable oil, place in the air fryer, prawn side up, and cook for 8–10 minutes, until golden.

 IF COOKING NOW

Follow the method in the 'making ahead to freeze' section up until the end of step 3.

HOB

Heat a good glug of vegetable oil in a non-stick frying pan on a medium heat. Once hot, add the prawn toasts, prawn side down, and cook in batches for 2–3 minutes on each side, until golden.

AIR FRYER

Preheat the air fryer to 180°C. Drizzle the prawn toasts with a little vegetable oil, place in the air fryer, prawn side up, and cook for 8–10 minutes, until golden.

TIP

Serve sprinkled with chopped chives, and with sweet chilli sauce to dip the toasts into!

SOY CHILLI BEEF & PEPPERS

This super easy recipe takes 5 minutes to make up and is packed full of delicious flavour. I like to make two up at once and have a spare full meal in the freezer for whenever we fancy a fakeaway at home.

Prep: 5 minutes | **Serves:** 4

1 red pepper, deseeded and finely sliced

1 green pepper, deseeded and finely sliced

1 onion, finely sliced

2 tsp frozen chopped ginger

2 tsp frozen chopped garlic

½ cup (120ml) soy sauce

2 tbsp sweet chilli sauce

1 tsp cornflour

¼ cup (60ml) tomato ketchup

2 tbsp rice wine vinegar

1 tsp frozen chopped chilli

750g diced stewing beef

To cook:
1 tbsp vegetable oil

½ cup (120ml) boiling water

 ## IF MAKING AHEAD TO FREEZE

1 Put everything apart from the diced beef into a large labelled freezer bag and mix.

2 Put the beef into a separate freezer bag, then seal and place inside the larger bag. Seal and freeze flat.

 ### HOB

Remove from the freezer and leave to fully defrost. Place a casserole dish on the hob on a high heat and add a tablespoon of oil. Add the beef and brown all over in batches. Once all the beef is browned, add the rest of the ingredients. Pour over the boiling water, bring to the boil and stir, then pop the lid on and leave to cook on a low heat for 3 hours, until the beef is tender.

SLOW COOKER

Remove from the freezer and leave to fully defrost. Turn the slow cooker on to the sauté setting. Add a tablespoon of oil and brown the beef all over in batches. Once all the beef is browned, add the rest of the ingredients to the slow cooker and mix. Pour over the boiling water, give everything a good stir, then pop the lid on and cook for 4 hours on high, or 8 hours on low, until the beef is tender.

PRESSURE COOKER

Remove from the freezer and leave to fully defrost. Turn the pressure cooker on to the sauté setting. Add a tablespoon of oil and brown the beef all over in batches. Once all the beef is browned, add the rest of the ingredients to the pressure cooker and mix. Pour over the boiling water, give everything a good stir, seal the lid and cook on high pressure for 15 minutes, then allow to naturally release.

 ## IF COOKING NOW

 ### HOB

Place a casserole dish on the hob on a high heat and add a tablespoon of oil. Add the beef and brown all over in batches. Once all the beef is browned, add the rest of the ingredients, stir well, then pour over the boiling water. Bring to the boil, then pop the lid on and leave to cook on a low heat for 3 hours, until the beef is tender.

 ### SLOW COOKER

Turn the slow cooker on to the sauté setting. Add a tablespoon of oil and brown the beef all over in batches. Once all the beef is browned, add the rest of the ingredients to the slow cooker and mix. Pour over the boiling water, give everything a good stir, then pop the lid on and cook for 4 hours on high, or 8 hours on low, until the beef is tender.

 ### PRESSURE COOKER

Turn the pressure cooker on to the sauté setting. Add a tablespoon of oil and brown the beef all over in batches. Once all the beef is browned, add the rest of the ingredients to the pressure cooker and mix. Pour over the boiling water, give everything a good stir, seal the lid and cook on high pressure for 15 minutes, then allow to naturally release.

TIP
Serve with fluffy rice or noodles and some prawn crackers, with sliced spring onion sprinkled on top to garnish.

TEX MEX BURGER

This is the ultimate Friday night burger! It brings all the flavours of Tex Mex into one big burger with an oozy Mexican cheese centre.

Prep: 5 minutes | **Makes:** 4

500g beef mince (with at least 10% fat)

1 small onion, very finely diced

2 tbsp yellow American-style mustard

1 egg

2 tbsp fajita seasoning

½ tsp chipotle paste

a small handful of jalapeños from a jar, drained and finely diced (optional)

50g Mexican cheese (also known as Cheddar with chilli), cut into 4 cubes

To cook:
vegetable oil

 IF MAKING AHEAD TO FREEZE

1   Put all the burger ingredients apart from the cheese into a large bowl. Mix with your hands to combine well, then tip onto a work surface. Split the mix into 4, then roll each piece into a ball.
2   Slightly flatten each ball, place a cube of Mexican cheese in the middle, then close the meat around the cheese and press down slightly to give you a thick burger patty. Repeat to make the other 3 burgers.
3   Put the burgers into a large labelled freezer bag and freeze flat.

HOB

Remove the burgers from the freezer and leave them to fully defrost. Heat a splash of oil in a frying pan on a medium heat and cook the burgers for 6–7 minutes on each side, until cooked through.

AIR FRYER

Remove the burgers from the freezer and leave them to fully defrost. Preheat the air fryer to 180°C. Cook the burgers in the air fryer for 14 minutes, flipping them over halfway through.

 IF COOKING NOW

Follow the method in the 'making ahead to freeze' section up until the end of step 2.

HOB

Heat a splash of oil in a frying pan on a medium heat and cook the burgers for 6–7 minutes on each side, until cooked through.

AIR FRYER

Preheat the air fryer to 180°C. Cook the burgers in the air fryer for 14 minutes, flipping them over halfway through.

TIP

Serve in buns with lots of tomato salsa, mayonnaise, lettuce and some tortilla chips.

SLOW-COOKED CHIPOTLE CHICKEN & BLACK BEANS

This is the most delicious and easy slow-cooked chicken recipe! It is a proper crowd-pleaser and it's brilliant to serve if you have lots of people coming over. I like to serve it with taco shells or tortillas and all the sides!

Prep: 5 minutes | **Serves:** 4

6 skinless and boneless chicken thighs

2 tsp frozen chopped garlic

½ cup (120ml) barbecue sauce

1 tsp onion granules

2 tsp chipotle paste

1 tsp smoked paprika

1 tbsp white wine vinegar

1 chicken stock cube, crumbled

1 x 400g tin of black beans, drained and rinsed

To cook:
½ cup (120ml) boiling water

 ## IF MAKING AHEAD TO FREEZE

1 Put the chicken thighs, garlic, barbecue sauce, onion granules, chipotle paste, smoked paprika, vinegar and crumbled stock cube into a large labelled freezer bag. Mix well.

2 Put the drained black beans into a smaller freezer bag, seal and slot inside the larger freezer bag containing the chicken. Seal and freeze flat.

OVEN

Remove from the freezer and fully defrost. Preheat the oven to 160°C. Pour the chicken mix into an ovenproof dish, add the boiling water, cover with tin foil and place in the oven for 1 hour. Remove the foil and shred the chicken using two forks, then stir through the black beans and return to the oven for 20 minutes, uncovered.

SLOW COOKER

Remove from the freezer and fully defrost. Pour the chicken mix into the slow cooker, add the boiling water, pop the lid on and cook for 3 hours on high, or 6 hours on low. Once cooked, shred the chicken using two forks and stir through the drained black beans. Cover and cook for a final 20 minutes on high.

PRESSURE COOKER

Remove from the freezer and fully defrost. Put the chicken mix into the pressure cooker with the boiling water. Seal the lid and cook on high pressure for 15 minutes. Once cooked, quickly release the pressure and open the lid. Shred the chicken using two forks, stir through the black beans and cook on the sauté setting for 10 minutes.

 ## IF COOKING NOW

OVEN

Preheat the oven to 160°C. Put the chicken thighs, garlic, barbecue sauce, onion granules, chipotle paste, smoked paprika, vinegar and crumbled stock cube into an ovenproof dish. Add the boiling water, cover with tin foil and place in the oven for 1 hour. Remove the foil and shred the chicken using two forks, then stir through the black beans and cook for another 20 minutes, uncovered.

SLOW COOKER

Put the chicken thighs, garlic, barbecue sauce, onion granules, chipotle paste, smoked paprika, vinegar and crumbled stock cube into the slow cooker, add the boiling water, pop the lid on and cook for 3 hours on high, or 6 hours on low. Once cooked, shred the chicken using two forks and stir through the drained black beans. Cover and cook for a final 20 minutes on high.

PRESSURE COOKER

Put the chicken thighs, garlic, barbecue sauce, onion granules, chipotle paste, smoked paprika, vinegar and crumbled stock cube into the pressure cooker, add the boiling water, seal the lid and cook on high pressure for 15 minutes. Once cooked, quickly release the pressure and open the lid. Shred the chicken using two forks, stir through the black beans and cook on the sauté setting for 10 minutes.

TIP
Serve with taco shells or tortillas, soured cream, pickled red onion and avocado!

PORK CARNITAS

This slow-cooked Mexican-style pork is so good! Once shredded, it can be used for all sorts, but I love to put it in taco shells or tortillas or make enchiladas for a delicious meal. This fakeaway recipe is perfect for serving to a crowd, as it serves at least 8.

Prep: 5–10 minutes | **Serves:** 8

2 tsp dried oregano

1 tsp dried thyme

2 tsp ground cumin

1 tsp garlic powder

2 tsp smoked paprika

1 tbsp light brown sugar

2 tsp frozen chopped garlic

1 pork or chicken stock cube, crumbled

2 tbsp vegetable oil

2 tsp salt

1.5kg boneless pork shoulder, excess fat trimmed off

2 onions, sliced

1 cup (240ml) orange juice

To cook:
¼ cup (60ml) boiling water

 **IF MAKING AHEAD TO FREEZE**

1. Put all the herbs and spices into a small bowl with the sugar, garlic, stock cube, oil and salt, and mix into a paste.
2. Place the pork shoulder on a board and rub it all over with the spice paste.
3. Put the pork shoulder and sliced onions into a very large labelled freezer bag, then pour over the orange juice, give the bag a good shake, seal and freeze flat.

OVEN

Remove from the freezer and leave to fully defrost. Preheat the oven to 160°C. Tip everything into a roasting tin and pour over the boiling water. Cover with tin foil and place in the oven for 4 hours. Remove the pork and shred it using two forks, then put it back into the oven without the foil for a further 30 minutes, to crisp up.

SLOW COOKER

Remove from the freezer and leave to fully defrost. Put everything into the slow cooker along with the boiling water, then pop the lid on and cook for 5–6 hours on high, or 9–10 hours on low. Once the meat is very soft, pull it apart using two forks, transfer to a baking tray and finish under a hot grill for 7–8 minutes, to crisp up.

 IF COOKING NOW

Follow the method in the 'making ahead to freeze' section up until the end of step 1.

OVEN

Preheat the oven to 160°C. Put the pork and onions into a large roasting tin and rub the pork all over with the spice paste. Pour in the orange juice and boiling water. Cover with tin foil and place in the oven for 4 hours. Remove the pork, then shred it using two forks and return it to the oven without the foil for a further 30 minutes, to crisp up.

SLOW COOKER

Put the pork and onions into the slow cooker. Rub the spice paste all over the pork, then pour in the orange juice and boiling water. Pop the lid on and cook for 5–6 hours on high, or 9–10 hours on low. Once the meat is very soft, pull it apart using two forks, transfer to a baking tray and finish off under a hot grill for 7–8 minutes, to crisp up.

TIP

I like to serve these in taco shells or brioche buns, with some coleslaw.

HONEY SESAME CHICKEN

This super easy chicken recipe is the perfect mix of sweet and savoury.
I love to serve it over fluffy rice for that takeaway feel at home.

Prep: 5 minutes | **Serves:** 4

8 skinless and boneless
chicken thighs

1 cup (115g) frozen diced
onions

2 tsp frozen chopped garlic

2 tsp frozen chopped
ginger

½ cup (120ml) runny honey

⅔ cup (180ml) soy sauce

½ tsp chilli flakes

2 tbsp sesame oil

3 tbsp sesame seeds

2 tsp cornflour

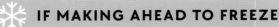 ❄ **IF MAKING AHEAD TO FREEZE**

Put everything into a large labelled freezer bag, mix and freeze flat.

HOB

Remove from the freezer and leave to
fully defrost. Pour everything into a large
saucepan and place on a medium heat.
Bring to the boil, then reduce the heat to
a simmer and cook for 30–35 minutes,
stirring every so often.

SLOW COOKER

Remove from the freezer and leave
to fully defrost. Put the contents of the
freezer bag into the slow cooker, pop
the lid on and cook for 4 hours on high,
or 6 hours on low.

IF COOKING NOW

HOB

Put everything into a large saucepan,
stir and place it on a medium heat.
Bring to the boil, then reduce the heat
to a simmer and cook for 30–35 minutes,
stirring every so often.

SLOW COOKER

Put everything into the slow cooker, stir,
pop the lid on and cook for 4 hours on
high, or 6 hours on low.

TIP
*Serve with fluffy rice
and vegetables.*

CURRYWURST

If you've ever been to Germany you will have probably seen this hugely popular late-night street food! This recipe is a super quick version, using smoked sausage, and it works brilliantly!

Prep: 5 minutes | **Serves:** 4

1 cup (115g) frozen diced onions

1 tsp frozen chopped garlic

½ cup (120ml) tomato ketchup

1 tbsp apple cider vinegar

1 tbsp yellow American-style mustard

1 tsp smoked paprika

2 tbsp curry powder

1 beef stock cube, crumbled

2 tsp Worcestershire sauce

2 x 160g ready-to-eat cooked smoked sausages, cut into thick slices

To cook:
1¼ cups (300ml) boiling water

 ❄ **IF MAKING AHEAD TO FREEZE**

Put everything into a large labelled freezer bag and mix. Before freezing, use the divided freezing method on pages 21–22 to ensure that your frozen meal will fit into your pot or slow cooker. Seal and freeze flat.

 **HOB**

Put the frozen currywurst into a large saucepan and place on a low-medium heat. Add the boiling water and break up with a spoon as it begins to defrost. Bring to the boil, then reduce to a simmer and cook for 20–25 minutes, stirring regularly, until the sauce has thickened slightly.

SLOW COOKER

Put the frozen currywurst into the slow cooker along with the boiling water, break up slightly with a spoon, then pop the lid on and cook for 3–4 hours on high, or 6–7 hours on low.

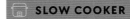 **IF COOKING NOW**

HOB

Put all the ingredients into a large saucepan and place on a medium heat. Add the boiling water, stir and bring to the boil, then reduce to a simmer and cook for 15–20 minutes, stirring regularly, until the sauce has thickened slightly.

SLOW COOKER

Put all the ingredients into the slow cooker along with the boiling water. Mix well, pop the lid on, then cook for 3 hours on high, or 6 hours on low.

TIP
Serve with crunchy oven-baked chips and an extra little sprinkle of curry powder.

FAMILY
—— & ——
FRIENDS

INDIVIDUAL SALMON EN CROÛTE

A traditional salmon en croûte is made with a whole side of salmon and feeds many people. These individual croûtes are made to be single portions, so you can grab however many you need from the freezer and pop them straight into the oven.

Prep: 10–15 minutes | **Serves:** 4

4 heaped tbsp crème fraîche

a handful of fresh dill, finely chopped

2 tbsp capers, drained and roughly chopped (optional)

a large handful of fresh parsley, finely chopped

1 cup (140g) frozen peas

zest and juice of 1 lemon

salt and pepper

2 sheets of ready-rolled puff pastry

4 skinless salmon fillets (approx. 130g each)

1 egg, beaten

 IF MAKING AHEAD TO FREEZE

1 Put the crème fraîche, dill, capers (if using), parsley, peas and lemon zest and juice into a mixing bowl. Season with salt and pepper and combine.
2 Unroll the sheets of puff pastry and cut each sheet into quarters, giving you 8 large rectangles.
3 On one sheet, distribute the creamy pea mix between the 4 rectangles, spreading it out but leaving a 2.5cm gap round the sides. Lay a salmon fillet over each filling.

4 With the other sheet, use the pastry rectangles to top each salmon fillet and enclose the filling. Using a fork, crimp round the edge of each parcel to stick the edges of the pastry together and enclose the filling.
5 Brush the top of each parcel with the beaten egg.
6 Wrap each parcel up in tin foil, then put them into a large labelled freezer bag and freeze flat.

 OVEN

Preheat the oven to 180°C. Unwrap the frozen croûtes, place them on a lined baking tray, and cook for 45–50 minutes, until golden. Cover with tin foil if browning too quickly.

AIR FRYER

Preheat the air fryer to 175°C. Unwrap the frozen croûtes, place in the air fryer and cook for 30–35 minutes, flipping them over halfway through, until golden.

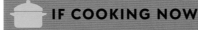 **IF COOKING NOW**

Follow the method in the 'making ahead to freeze' section up until the end of step 5.

OVEN

Preheat the oven to 180°C. Place the croûtes on a lined baking tray and cook for 30–35 minutes, until golden.

AIR FRYER

Preheat the air fryer to 175°C. Place the croûtes in the air fryer and cook them for 25 minutes, flipping them over halfway through, until golden.

TIP

Serve with a lovely fresh salad and some buttery new potatoes.

BARBECUE CHICKEN KING KEBAB

This sharing-style chicken kebab is the ultimate Friday night feast, so get some friends round and enjoy! It is also brilliant cooked on the barbecue, so it's great for a summer party. For this recipe, you will need four long wooden or metal skewers.

Prep: 5 minutes | **Serves:** 4

8 skinless and boneless chicken thighs

2 tbsp light brown sugar

1 tbsp smoked paprika

1 tsp salt

1 tsp garlic powder

1 tsp dried thyme

2 tsp Dijon mustard

½ cup (120ml) barbecue sauce

2 tbsp cider vinegar

 IF MAKING AHEAD TO FREEZE

Put everything into a large labelled freezer bag, mix together and freeze flat.

OVEN

Remove from the freezer and leave to fully defrost. Preheat the grill. Thread four of the chicken thighs on two skewers, running parallel through the outer edges of the chicken, making sure they are not tightly packed together. Repeat with the remaining chicken thighs. Place on a grill pan under the grill and cook for 12–14 minutes on each side. Make sure the chicken is fully cooked, then remove the skewers, slice and serve.

AIR FRYER

Remove from the freezer and leave to fully defrost. Preheat the air fryer to 180°C. Thread four of the chicken thighs on two skewers, running parallel through the outer edges of the chicken, making sure they are not tightly packed together. Repeat with the remaining chicken thighs. Cook in the air fryer for 25–30 minutes, flipping them over halfway through. Make sure the chicken is fully cooked, then remove the skewers, slice and serve.

 IF COOKING NOW

Put everything into a large bowl and mix well. Leave to marinate for 15 minutes.

OVEN

Preheat the grill. Thread four of the chicken thighs on two skewers, running parallel through the outer edges of the chicken, making sure they are not tightly packed together. Repeat with the remaining chicken thighs. Place on a grill pan under the grill and cook for 12–14 minutes on each side. Make sure the chicken is fully cooked, then remove the skewers, slice and serve.

AIR FRYER

Preheat the air fryer to 180°C. Thread four of the chicken thighs on two skewers, running parallel through the outer edges of the chicken, making sure they are not tightly packed together. Repeat with the remaining chicken thighs. Cook in the air fryer for 25–30 minutes, flipping them over halfway through. Make sure the chicken is fully cooked, then remove the skewers, slice and serve.

TIP

Serve with corn on the hob, coleslaw, potato wedges and extra barbecue sauce.

COQ AU VIN

This is a classic French dish that is brilliant for feeding lots of people. Served with mashed potatoes and seasonal veggies, it is the perfect dinner party or Sunday lunch recipe for any time of year. The browning of the chicken and lardons gives all the flavour, so don't miss out this step!

Prep: 5 minutes | **Serves:** 4

4 bone-in chicken legs

1 x 125g pack of smoked bacon lardons

1 cup (115g) frozen diced onions

250g mushrooms, sliced

4 tsp frozen chopped garlic

2 celery sticks, finely diced

1 medium carrot, peeled and cut into chunks

2 tbsp tomato purée

2 bay leaves

1 chicken stock cube, crumbled

2 tbsp plain flour

½ cup (120ml) red wine

To cook:

1 tbsp olive oil

1½ cups (360ml) boiling water

 IF MAKING AHEAD TO FREEZE

1 Put the chicken legs and lardons into a very large labelled freezer bag.

2 Put the rest of the ingredients into a smaller freezer bag and place inside the bag of chicken legs and lardons.

3 Seal and freeze flat.

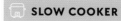

HOB

Remove from the freezer and leave to fully defrost. Put 1 tablespoon of oil into a large, deep-sided frying pan or casserole dish and place on a high heat. Add the chicken legs and lardons and brown all over, until golden. Add the rest of the ingredients and the boiling water, mix well and bring to the boil, then reduce the heat to a simmer. Pop the lid on and cook for 2 hours.

SLOW COOKER

Remove from the freezer and leave to fully defrost. Put 1 tablespoon of oil into the slow cooker and turn it on to the sauté setting. Add the chicken legs and lardons and brown all over, until golden – you may need to do this in batches. Add the rest of the ingredients and the boiling water, mix well, then pop the lid on and cook for 3–4 hours on high, or 7–8 hours on low.

PRESSURE COOKER

Remove from the freezer and leave to fully defrost. Put 1 tablespoon of oil into the pressure cooker and turn it on to the sauté setting. Add the chicken legs and lardons and brown all over, until golden – you may need to do this in batches. Add the rest of the ingredients and the boiling water, mix well. Seal the lid, cook on high pressure for 16 minutes, then quickly release.

 IF COOKING NOW

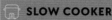

HOB

Put 1 tablespoon of oil into a large, deep-sided frying pan or casserole dish and place on a high heat. Add the chicken legs and lardons and brown all over, until golden. Add the rest of the ingredients and the boiling water, mix and bring to the boil, then reduce the heat to a simmer. Pop the lid on and cook for 2 hours.

SLOW COOKER

Put 1 tablespoon of oil into the slow cooker and turn it on to the sauté setting. Add the chicken legs and lardons and brown all over, until golden – you may need to do this in batches. Add the rest of the ingredients and the boiling water and mix well. Pop the lid on and cook for 3–4 hours on high, or 7–8 hours on low.

PRESSURE COOKER

Put 1 tablespoon of oil into the pressure cooker and turn it on to the sauté setting. Add the chicken legs and lardons and brown all over until golden – you may need to do this in batches. Add the rest of the ingredients and the boiling water, mix well. Seal the lid, cook on high pressure for 16 minutes, then quickly release.

TIP

Serve with mashed potatoes and seasonal veggies.

LAMB KLEFTIKO

This delicious spiced lamb dish is a real taste of Greece. It is slow-cooked, so the lamb is beautifully tender and melts in the mouth. This is a one-pot meal with all the veggies and potatoes included, making it a simple and easy crowd-pleaser.

Prep: 5–10 minutes | **Serves:** 4–6

2 tbsp olive oil

juice of 1 lemon

1 tbsp runny honey

6 tsp frozen chopped garlic

2 tbsp dried oregano

2 tbsp dried rosemary

1 chicken or lamb stock cube, crumbled

2 tsp salt

1 x 1.2kg joint of boneless lamb shoulder

2 red peppers, deseeded and sliced

2 onions, cut into rough chunks

600g new potatoes, halved

1 x 200g pack of feta cheese

To cook:
1 cup (240ml) boiling water

 ## IF MAKING AHEAD TO FREEZE

1 Put the olive oil, lemon juice, honey, garlic, oregano, rosemary, crumbled stock cube and salt into a very large labelled freezer bag and mix together.
2 Add the lamb shoulder to the bag and coat in the marinade, then add the red peppers, onions and potatoes.
3 Crumble the feta into a small freezer bag, seal and slot it inside the larger bag, then seal and freeze flat.

 ### OVEN

Remove from the freezer and leave to fully defrost (this may take up to 24 hours). Preheat the oven to 150°C. Put the vegetables in a lidded casserole dish and lay the lamb on top. Pour in the boiling water, then cover first with a sheet of baking parchment and then with a sheet of tin foil on top, seal really well and pop the lid on. Place in the oven for 3½ hours, then remove from the oven and shred the lamb with two forks. Mix through the vegetables and sprinkle over the feta, then cook, uncovered, for 45 minutes.

SLOW COOKER

Remove from the freezer and leave to fully defrost (this may take up to 24 hours). Put the vegetables in the bottom of the slow cooker and lay the lamb on top. Pour in the boiling water and put the lid on. Cook for 5 hours on high, or 9 hours on low, then shred the lamb with two forks. Mix through the vegetables and sprinkle over the feta, put the lid on and cook for a further 15 minutes on high.

 ## IF COOKING NOW

Put the olive oil, lemon juice, honey, garlic, oregano, rosemary, crumbled stock cube and salt into a small bowl and mix together to make a marinade.

 ### OVEN

Preheat the oven to 150°C. Put the vegetables in a lidded casserole dish and lay the lamb on top. Pour the marinade over the lamb, rubbing it all over. Pour in the boiling water, then cover first with a sheet of baking parchment and then with a sheet of tin foil on top, seal really well and pop the lid on. Place in the oven for 3½ hours, then remove from the oven and shred the lamb with two forks. Mix through the vegetables and sprinkle over the feta, then cook, uncovered, for 45 minutes.

SLOW COOKER

Put the red peppers, onions and new potatoes in the bottom of the slow cooker and lay the lamb on top. Pour the marinade over the lamb, rubbing it all over. Pour in the boiling water and put the lid on. Cook for 5 hours on high, or 9 hours on low, then shred the lamb with two forks. Mix through the vegetables and sprinkle over the feta, put the lid on and cook for a further 15 minutes on high.

TIP
I like to serve this with fresh mint on top.

TERIYAKI BEEF KEBABS

These kebabs are so easy to make and work brilliantly if you have lots of people over. Why not pair them with the Paneer Kebabs on page 178, for a great weekend feast with friends? For this recipe, you will need six wooden or metal skewers.

Prep: 5–10 minutes | **Makes:** 6

3 tbsp soy sauce

a large knob of fresh ginger, finely grated

2 cloves of garlic, grated

1 tbsp runny honey

1 tbsp sesame oil

1 tbsp rice wine vinegar

1 tsp cornflour

400g sirloin beef steak, cut into 6 long strips

 ## IF MAKING AHEAD TO FREEZE

1 Put everything apart from the beef into a large mixing bowl and stir to combine.

2 Add the beef to the bowl and mix again.

3 Pour into a large labelled freezer bag and freeze flat.

 ### OVEN

Remove from the freezer and leave to fully defrost. Preheat the grill. Thread the beef strips on skewers lengthways, weaving back and forth. Place on a grill pan and grill for 2–3 minutes on each side. Any marinade left in the bag can be reheated in a saucepan and poured over the cooked beef.

 ### AIR FRYER

Remove from the freezer and leave to fully defrost. Preheat the air fryer to 210°C. Thread the beef strips on skewers lengthways, weaving back and forth. Cook in the air fryer for 3 minutes, flip over and cook for a further 1 minute. Any marinade left in the bag can be reheated in a pan and poured over the cooked beef.

 ## IF COOKING NOW

Follow the method in the 'making ahead to freeze' section up until the end of step 2.

 ### OVEN

Preheat the grill. Thread the beef strips on skewers lengthways, weaving back and forth. Place on a grill pan and grill for 2–3 minutes on each side. Any leftover marinade can be reheated in a saucepan and poured over the cooked beef.

 ### AIR FRYER

Preheat the air fryer to 210°C. Thread the beef strips on skewers lengthways, weaving back and forth. Cook in the air fryer for 3 minutes, then flip over and cook for a further 1 minute. Any leftover marinade can be reheated in a saucepan and poured over the cooked beef.

TIP

Serve with steamed rice, finely sliced spring onions and a good sprinkle of sesame seeds.

PANEER KEBABS

Paneer is an Indian cheese and works wonderfully when threaded on kebab sticks. This recipe also uses lots of delicious veggies and a lovely yoghurt spice blend. Why not pair these with the Teriyaki Beef Kebabs on page 176 for a great weekend feast with friends? For this recipe, you will need four metal or wooden kebab skewers.

Prep: 5 minutes | **Serves:** 4

½ cup (110g) Greek yoghurt

2 tsp frozen chopped garlic

2 tsp frozen chopped ginger

1 tbsp medium curry powder

1 tsp ground turmeric

1 tbsp vegetable oil

1 tsp salt

500g paneer cheese, cut into 3cm cubes

1 green pepper, deseeded and cut into thick chunks

1 red pepper, deseeded and cut into thick chunks

2 red onions, cut into thick chunks

❄️ IF MAKING AHEAD TO FREEZE

1   Put the yoghurt, garlic, ginger, curry powder, turmeric, vegetable oil and salt into a large mixing bowl. Mix together to make a marinade.

2   Add the paneer chunks, peppers and onions and mix well.

3   Pour everything into a large labelled freezer bag and freeze flat.

OVEN

Remove from the freezer and leave to fully defrost. Preheat the grill. Thread the paneer, peppers and onions on the skewers, dividing the ingredients between them. Place under the hot grill for 10 minutes, flipping them over halfway through.

AIR FRYER

Remove from the freezer and leave to fully defrost. Preheat the air fryer to 190°C. Thread the paneer, peppers and onions on the skewers, dividing the ingredients between them. Cook in the air fryer for 10 minutes, flipping them over halfway through.

🍲 IF COOKING NOW

Follow the method in the 'making ahead to freeze' section up until the end of step 2.

OVEN

Preheat the grill. Thread the paneer, peppers and onions on the skewers, dividing the ingredients between them. Place under the hot grill for 10 minutes, flipping them over halfway through.

AIR FRYER

Preheat the air fryer to 190°C. Thread the paneer, peppers and onions on the skewers, dividing the ingredients between them. Cook in the air fryer for 10 minutes, flipping them over halfway through.

TIP

Serve the kebabs on hot naan bread, with a lovely side salad and a good drizzle of yoghurt and mango chutney.

TARRAGON CHICKEN WITH DUMPLINGS

This one-pot is the ultimate comforting dinner. It's filling, packed full of flavour and beautifully creamy. A great relaxing Sunday lunch recipe, best shared with friends and family.

Prep: 10–15 minutes | **Serves:** 4

For the dumplings:
scant 1 cup (100g) self-raising flour, plus extra for dusting

½ tsp salt

½ cup (60g) shredded vegetable suet

1 tbsp finely chopped fresh tarragon

6 tbsp cold water

For the chicken filling:
4 chicken breasts, each cut into 4 long strips

3 tsp frozen chopped garlic

1 large leek, thickly sliced

1 cup (140g) frozen peas

a handful of fresh tarragon, roughly chopped

1 tbsp Dijon mustard

1 chicken stock cube, crumbled

To cook:
1 cup (240ml) boiling water

½ cup (120ml) double cream

 IF MAKING AHEAD TO FREEZE

1 To make the dumplings, combine the flour, salt, suet and tarragon in a mixing bowl. Add the cold water and mix until it comes together to form a ball of dough. Tip out onto a lightly floured surface and cut the ball of dough in half, then cut each half into quarters, giving you 8 equal-sized pieces. Roll them into balls.

2 Place the rolled balls in a labelled freezer bag and seal.

3 Label a second large freezer bag, being sure to write on the bag that ½ cup (120ml) of double cream is needed on the day of cooking. Put all the chicken filling ingredients into the bag, mix, then seal and freeze flat alongside the dumplings.

 OVEN

Remove both freezer bags and leave to fully defrost. Preheat the oven to 180°C. Pour the chicken mix into a medium-sized, ovenproof dish, then pour over the boiling water, mix and cook for 35 minutes, until the chicken is cooked through. Remove from the oven, stir through the double cream, then place the dumplings on top and return to the oven for 20 minutes.

 SLOW COOKER

Remove both freezer bags and leave to fully defrost. Pour the chicken mix into the slow cooker, pour over the boiling water and mix. Pop the lid on and cook for 3 hours on high, or 6 hours on low. Stir through the double cream, then place the dumplings on top, pop the lid back on and cook for a further 1 hour on high.

 IF COOKING NOW

Follow the method in the 'making ahead to freeze section' up until the end of step 1.

OVEN

Preheat the oven to 180°C. Put all the chicken filling ingredients into a medium-sized, ovenproof dish, give it a mix, then add the boiling water. Mix again and cook for 35 minutes, until the chicken is cooked through. Remove from the oven, stir through the double cream and place the dumplings on top, then return to the oven for 20 minutes.

SLOW COOKER

Put all the chicken filling ingredients into the slow cooker, pour over the boiling water and mix. Pop the lid on and cook for 3 hours on high, or 6 hours on low. Stir through the double cream, then place the dumplings on top, pop the lid back on and cook for a further 1 hour on high.

TIP
Serve with spring greens and mashed potatoes.

SPRING VEGAN CRUNCH PIE

This springtime pie packed full of seasonal greens is such a winner, and a great main dish when you are having friends or family round. Like the sound of this but want to make it non-vegan? Simply swap the plant-based products for dairy.

Prep: 5–10 minutes | **Serves:** 4

100g sliced spring greens, a mix of kale and spring cabbage

150g frozen spinach (5 cubes), defrosted and excess water squeezed out

4 spring onions, finely sliced

2 tsp frozen chopped garlic

1 cup (140g) frozen peas

1 x 400g tin of butter beans, drained and rinsed

a large handful of fresh parsley, finely chopped

130g plant-based Boursin cheese

1 cup (250ml) plant-based double cream

salt and pepper

1 pack of filo pastry

To cook:
2 tbsp olive oil

❄️ IF MAKING AHEAD TO FREEZE

Put all the ingredients apart from the filo into a large bowl and mix well. Pour into a large labelled freezer bag and freeze flat alongside the pack of filo pastry.

⊞ OVEN

Remove from the freezer and leave to fully defrost. Preheat the oven to 180°C. Once defrosted, pour the mix into a saucepan and heat through on a low-medium heat for 10–12 minutes. Pour into a 20 x 30cm ovenproof dish. Loosely scrunch up 8 filo sheets one at a time and place them on top, to cover the pie mix. Drizzle with the olive oil and place in the oven for 15–20 minutes, until golden.

⊞ AIR FRYER

Remove from the freezer and leave to fully defrost. Preheat the air fryer to 175°C. Once defrosted, pour the mix into a saucepan and heat through on a low-medium heat for 10–12 minutes. Pour into a 20 x 30cm air fryer-safe dish. Loosely scrunch up 8 filo sheets one at a time and place them on top, to cover the pie mix. Drizzle with the olive oil and cook in the air fryer for 12–15 minutes, until golden.

🍲 IF COOKING NOW

⊞ OVEN

Preheat the oven to 180°C. Put all the ingredients apart from the filo into a large saucepan, mix well and heat through on a low-medium heat for 10–12 minutes. Pour into a 20 x 30cm ovenproof dish. Loosely scrunch up 8 filo sheets one at a time and place them on top, to cover the pie mix. Drizzle with the olive oil and place in the oven for 15–20 minutes, until golden.

⊞ AIR FRYER

Preheat the air fryer to 175°C. Put all the ingredients apart from the filo into a large saucepan, mix well and heat through on a low-medium heat for 10–12 minutes. Pour into a 20 x 30cm air fryer-safe dish. Loosely scrunch up 8 filo sheets one at a time and place them on top, covering the pie mix. Drizzle with oil and cook in the air fryer for 12–15 minutes, until golden.

TIP

Serve as it is, or with a side of new potatoes.

SAUSAGE JAMBALAYA

Jambalaya is a delicious rice-based one-pot stew. It is beautifully spiced and packed with lots of smoked sausage! This is a great easy one-pot for when you've got lots of family and friends over.

Prep: 5 minutes | **Serves:** 4

1 cup (115g) frozen diced onions

2 tsp frozen chopped garlic

160g ready-to-eat cooked smoked sausage, cut into chunks

2 cups (350g) frozen mixed sliced peppers

1 x 400g tin of chopped tomatoes

2 tbsp tomato purée

2 tsp Cajun seasoning

1 chicken stock cube, crumbled

1 cup (200g) white basmati rice, rinsed well

salt and pepper

To cook:
2 cups (480ml) boiling water

 IF MAKING AHEAD TO FREEZE

Put all the ingredients apart from the rice into a large labelled freezer bag and mix. Put the rice in a smaller freezer bag and seal, slot inside the larger bag, seal and freeze flat.

 HOB

Remove from the freezer and leave to fully defrost. Put the contents of both freezer bags into a large saucepan, cover with the boiling water and mix. Bring to the boil, then reduce to a simmer and cook for 20–25 minutes, stirring regularly.

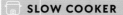 **SLOW COOKER**

Remove from the freezer and leave to fully defrost. Pour the contents of the larger freezer bag into the slow cooker and add the boiling water. Mix, pop the lid on and cook for 3–4 hours on high, or 7–8 hours on low. About 40 minutes before the end of the cooking time, stir in the rice, pop the lid back on and turn the slow cooker on to high if it is not already. Once the rice is tender, serve.

 IF COOKING NOW

HOB

Put everything into a large saucepan, cover with the boiling water and stir. Bring to the boil, then reduce to a simmer and cook for 20–25 minutes, stirring regularly.

SLOW COOKER

Put everything apart from the rice into the slow cooker, cover with the boiling water and stir. Pop the lid on and cook for 3–4 hours on high, or 7–8 hours on low. When you have 40 minutes before the end of the cooking time, stir in the rice, pop the lid back on and turn the slow cooker on to high if it is not already. Once the rice is tender, serve up.

TIP

To make this vegan, use a plant-based smoked sausage and a vegetable stock cube.

MARINATED SPATCHCOCK CHICKEN

This is one of my favourite recipes – it's the perfect centrepiece for a Sunday lunch with friends. It's also great cooked on the barbecue when the sun comes out! Spatchcocking a chicken is a brilliant way of getting the chicken to cook quicker.

Prep: 10–15 minutes | **Serves:** 6

1¼ cups (300ml) buttermilk

zest of 1 lemon

4 cloves of garlic, grated

2 tbsp dried oregano

1 tsp chilli flakes

1 tsp dried thyme

2 tsp salt

a good grind of pepper

1 large oven-ready chicken (approx. 1.6kg)

IF MAKING AHEAD TO FREEZE

1 Put the buttermilk, lemon zest, garlic, oregano, chilli flakes, thyme, salt and a good grind of pepper into a very large labelled freezer bag and mix.

2 To spatchcock the chicken, turn it over so it is upside down and the legs are pointing towards you, on a chopping board. Using extra sharp scissors, cut down each side of the backbone,

through the ribs and right to the end, then remove the backbone.

3 Turn the chicken back over, skin side up, and open it out. Using the palm of your hand, push the chicken down firmly so that it flattens.

4 Put the spatchocked chicken into the bag of marinade, mix well, then seal and freeze flat.

OVEN

Remove from the freezer and leave to fully defrost. Preheat the oven to 180°C. Place the chicken flat on a baking tray or ovenproof dish, skin side up, and cook for 45–50 minutes, until the chicken is cooked through.

AIR FRYER

Remove from the freezer and leave to fully defrost. Preheat the air fryer to 180°C. Place the chicken flat in the air fryer, skin side up, and cook for 35–40 minutes, flipping it over halfway, until the chicken is cooked through.

IF COOKING NOW

1 Follow the method in the 'making ahead to freeze section' up until the end of step 3, mixing the marinade ingredients in a very large bowl.

2 Add the chicken to the bowl of marinade, rub all over, then leave to sit for 20 minutes.

OVEN

Preheat the oven to 180°C. Place the chicken flat on a baking tray or ovenproof dish, skin side up, and cook for 45–50 minutes, until the chicken is cooked through.

AIR FRYER

Preheat the air fryer to 180°C. Place the chicken flat in the air fryer, skin side up, and cook for 35–40 minutes, flipping it over halfway, until the chicken is cooked through.

TIP
Serve with a salad, chips and an aïoli dip.

COCONUT, SPINACH & TOMATO DHAL

Dhal is a wonderfully easy dish to make for lots of people. It's creamy, fresh and packed full of goodness.

Prep: 5 minutes | **Serves:** 4–6

1¾ cups (350g) dried red lentils, rinsed well

1 cup (115g) frozen diced onions

3 tsp frozen chopped garlic

2 tsp frozen chopped ginger

1 tsp ground turmeric

1 tbsp medium curry powder

100g fresh spinach or 4 cubes of frozen spinach

1 x 400g tin of chopped tomatoes

1 x 400ml tin of coconut milk

1 vegetable stock cube, crumbled

a large handful of fresh coriander, finely chopped

juice of 1 lemon

To cook:
3 cups (720ml) boiling water

TIP

Serve with naan bread and yoghurt (use plant-based if cooking for vegans) and chopped fresh coriander.

❄ IF MAKING AHEAD TO FREEZE

Put all the ingredients into a large labelled freezer bag and mix. Use the divided freezing method on pages 21–22, to ensure it'll fit into the pot or slow cooker. Freeze flat.

HOB

Put the frozen dhal mix into a saucepan with the boiling water. Place on a low-medium heat to defrost, breaking it down with the back of a spoon. Once defrosted, bring to the boil, reduce to a simmer and cook for 40 minutes, stirring regularly until the lentils are tender, adding a splash of water if needed.

SLOW COOKER

Put the frozen dhal mix into the slow cooker along with the boiling water, pop the lid on and cook for 5 hours on high, or 8 hours on low, giving it a stir after 1 hour and cooking until the lentils are tender.

PRESSURE COOKER

Put the frozen dhal mix into the pressure cooker with the boiling water. Turn it on to the sauté setting and break the mix up with the back of a spoon as it starts to defrost. After 10 minutes, seal the lid and cook on high pressure for 12 minutes, then allow it to naturally release for 10 minutes.

IF COOKING NOW

HOB

Put everything into a saucepan along with the boiling water and mix. Bring to the boil, then reduce to a simmer and cook for 30–35 minutes, stirring regularly until the lentils are tender, adding a splash of water if needed.

SLOW COOKER

Put everything into the slow cooker along with the boiling water. Mix well, pop the lid on and cook for 4 hours on high, or 8 hours on low, until the lentils are tender.

PRESSURE COOKER

Put everything into the pressure cooker along with the boiling water. Mix well, seal the lid and cook on high pressure for 12 minutes, and then allow it to naturally release for 10 minutes.

SLOW-COOKED KOREAN-STYLE BEEF

I love the Korean-inspired flavours in this one-pot, the beef is seriously tender and it is super easy to make!

Prep: 5 minutes | **Serves:** 4

1kg diced stewing beef

¼ cup (60ml) soy sauce

5 tsp frozen chopped garlic

3 tbsp sesame oil

2 tbsp light brown sugar

1 red onion, finely diced

1 beef stock cube, crumbled

1 tbsp cornflour

To cook:
1 tbsp oil

1 cup (240ml) boiling water

 ## IF MAKING AHEAD TO FREEZE

1 Put the diced beef into a large labelled freezer bag.

2 Put all the other ingredients into a smaller freezer bag, mix and seal. Place the small freezer bag inside the bag of beef. Seal and freeze flat.

 ### HOB

Remove from the freezer and leave to fully defrost. Heat the oil in a large casserole dish, then add the beef and brown in batches. Once the meat is browned, add the rest of the ingredients and the boiling water. Mix well and bring to the boil, then reduce to a simmer and leave to cook for 3 hours.

SLOW COOKER

Remove from the freezer and leave to fully defrost. Put the oil into the slow cooker and turn on to the sauté setting. Add the beef and brown all over in batches. Once the meat is browned, add the rest of the ingredients and the boiling water. Mix well, pop the lid on and cook for 4 hours on high, or 8 hours on low.

PRESSURE COOKER

Remove from the freezer and leave to fully defrost. Put the oil into the pressure cooker and turn on to the sauté setting. Add the beef and brown all over in batches. Once the meat is browned, add the rest of the ingredients and the boiling water. Mix well, then close the lid and turn on to the high pressure setting. Cook for 15 minutes, then allow it to naturally release.

 ## IF COOKING NOW

 ### HOB

Heat the oil in a large casserole dish, then add the beef and brown in batches. Once the meat is browned, add the rest of the ingredients and the boiling water. Mix well and bring to the boil, then reduce to a simmer and leave to cook for 3 hours.

 ### SLOW COOKER

Put the oil into the slow cooker and turn on to the sauté setting. Add the beef and brown all over in batches. Once the meat is browned, add the rest of the ingredients and the boiling water. Mix well, pop the lid on and cook for 4 hours on high, or 8 hours on low.

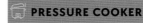 ### PRESSURE COOKER

Put the oil into the pressure cooker and turn on to the sauté setting. Add the beef and brown all over in batches. Once the meat is browned, add the rest of the ingredients and the boiling water. Mix well, then close the lid and turn on to the high pressure setting. Cook for 15 minutes, then allow it to naturally release.

TIP
Serve with fluffy rice, chopped spring onions and lots of sesame seeds.

EASY BAKES

APRICOT & ALMOND DANISH SWIRLS

Love the baked goods from your local coffee shop? Why not save money and make them at home! Brilliant to grab whenever you fancy a quick treat.

Prep: 10 minutes | **Makes:** 10

1 sheet of pre-rolled puff pastry

2 heaped tbsp cream cheese

3 heaped tbsp apricot jam

a handful of flaked almonds

For the icing glaze:

4 tbsp icing sugar

1–2 tsp cold water

a handful of flaked almonds

❄ IF MAKING AHEAD TO FREEZE

1 Unroll the puff pastry, keeping it on its paper.
2 Spread the cream cheese all over the pastry with a knife, leaving a 1cm border round the edges.
3 Carefully spread the apricot jam on top of the cream cheese, then sprinkle over the flaked almonds.
4 Working from a short end, using the paper to help, roll it into a tight roll.

Using a knife, cut the roll widthways in half and cut each half into 5 slices.
5 Open a large labelled freezer bag. Keeping the bag flat, put in the swirls, leaving space so they don't stick together. If you need to stack them on top of each other, make sure to add a sheet of baking parchment in between to stop them sticking. Place flat in the freezer until fully frozen.

▭ OVEN

Preheat the oven to 180°C. Place the frozen swirls on a lined baking tray and cook for 30–35 minutes, until golden, then remove and leave to cool.

▭ AIR FRYER

Preheat the air fryer to 180°C. Place the frozen swirls on baking parchment in the air fryer and cook for 18 minutes, flipping them over halfway through, until golden, then remove and leave to cool.

🍲 IF COOKING NOW

Follow the method in the 'making ahead to freeze' section up until the end of step 4.

▭ OVEN

Preheat the oven to 190°C. Cook the swirls on a lined baking tray for 25–30 minutes, until golden, then remove and leave to cool.

▭ AIR FRYER

Preheat the air fryer to 190°C. Place the swirls on baking parchment and cook in the air fryer for 16 minutes, flipping them over halfway through, until golden, then remove and leave to cool.

TIP

To make the icing glaze, put the icing sugar and cold water into a bowl. Mix well, then drizzle over the top of the cooked cool swirls and top with a few flaked almonds.

CARAMEL PEAR POCKETS

These pockets are so easy to make using cheat ingredients. No need to spend hours making caramel or pastry, simply follow this method for the most delicious snack, made at a fraction of the price of a shop-bought coffee-shop treat.

Prep: 10 minutes | **Makes:** 8

1 sheet of pre-rolled puff pastry

8 heaped tsp tinned caramel

1 x 210g tin of pear quarters, drained and diced into rough chunks

1 egg, beaten

1 tbsp demerara sugar

❄ IF MAKING AHEAD TO FREEZE

1 Unroll the puff pastry with a long side nearest to you, and cut into 8 even rectangles, by first cutting in half lengthways, then across the middle and then halving those again.

2 Each rectangle will be folded in half, so pop 1 teaspoon of caramel on the bottom half of each rectangle, then distribute the diced pear on top, evenly between the 8 pastries.

3 Brush the edge of the rectangles with the beaten egg, then fold the pastry over the top to enclose the filling.

4 Crimp round the edge of each pocket with a fork, pressing to stick the edges of the pastry together and enclose the filling inside.

5 Brush each pocket all over with the beaten egg, then sprinkle them with the demerara sugar.

6 Open a large labelled freezer bag. Keeping the bag flat, put in the uncooked pockets, leaving space between them so that they don't stick together. Place flat in the freezer until fully frozen.

🔲 OVEN

Preheat the oven to 180°C. Place the frozen pockets on a lined baking tray and cook for 20–25 minutes, until golden and puffed up.

AIR FRYER

Preheat the air fryer to 180°C. Put in the frozen pockets and cook for 12 minutes, flipping them over halfway through, until golden and puffed up.

🍲 IF COOKING NOW

Follow the method in the 'making ahead to freeze' section up until the end of step 5.

🔲 OVEN

Preheat the oven to 180°C. Place the pockets on a lined baking tray and cook for 20 minutes, until golden and puffed up.

AIR FRYER

Preheat the air fryer to 180°C and add the pockets. Cook for 9–10 minutes, flipping over halfway, until golden and puffed up.

TIP

To make this vegan, look for vegan puff pastry and caramel sauce, and use a little plant-based milk rather than a beaten egg.

COCONUT CHOCOLATE SLICE

You might remember making chocolate snowballs when you were younger
– these are very similar, but in a slice rather than a ball!

Prep: 10 minutes | **Makes:** 16

200g butter, at room temperature

¾ cup plus 2 heaped tbsp (200ml) condensed milk

1 tsp vanilla extract

2 tbsp cocoa powder

300g digestive biscuits

½ cup (50g) desiccated coconut

For the icing:
1½ cups (240g) icing sugar

4 tbsp cold water

¼ cup (30g) desiccated coconut

IF MAKING AHEAD TO FREEZE

1 Line a 20 x 20cm square tin with baking parchment.
2 Put the soft butter, condensed milk, vanilla extract and cocoa powder into a mixing bowl and mix with an electric whisk until smooth.
3 Blitz the digestives in a food processor or by putting them inside a freezer bag and bashing with a rolling pin, until you have fine crumbs. Add this to the bowl, along with the ½ cup (50g) of desiccated coconut. Combine really well until it all comes together into a soft dough.
4 Spread in the lined tin, using a spoon to smooth it out and press it into the edges. Place into the fridge for 1 hour.
5 When it has firmed up, remove from the fridge. Put the icing sugar into a bowl, add the water and mix until you have a smooth icing.
6 Spread the icing all over the top of the traybake and scatter over the ¼ cup (30g) of desiccated coconut.
7 Put back into the fridge for 20 minutes, then cut into 16 slices.
8 Place the slices in a large labelled freezer bag and freeze flat.

READY TO EAT

Remove the slices from the freezer and leave to defrost at room temperature for 1 hour before eating. These are best kept in the fridge once defrosted.

IF MAKING NOW

Follow the steps in the 'making ahead to freeze' section up until the end of step 7. It is ready to eat. This will keep in the fridge for up to 5 days in an airtight container.

TIP

To make this vegan, use plant-based butter and condensed milk.

CHOCOLATE CUSTARD TWISTS

These are the ultimate coffee dunker, and so delicious for breakfast or a weekend treat! Why not use any leftover custard to make the frozen custard on page 238?

Prep: 10 minutes | **Makes:** 8

1 sheet of pre-rolled puff pastry

2 heaped tbsp chocolate spread (I use Nutella)

3 heaped tbsp ready-made custard

1 egg, beaten

1 tbsp demerara sugar

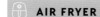 **IF MAKING AHEAD TO FREEZE**

1 Unroll the puff pastry with a long side nearest to you on the work surface. Cut down the middle to give you two equal halves.
2 Spread the chocolate spread all over one half, then spread the custard over the chocolate spread.
3 Lay the other half of the pastry on top, then, with a knife, cut into 8 long strips.
4 Take each strip and twist it by holding one end and twisting the other, you want to have 3–4 twists on each.
5 Brush each twist with beaten egg and sprinkle with demerara sugar.
6 Place on a lined tray and flash freeze for 1 hour, then place in a labelled freezer bag, seal and put back into the freezer.

OVEN

Preheat the oven to 180°C. Put the frozen twists on a lined baking tray and cook for 20–22 minutes.

AIR FRYER

Preheat the air fryer to 180°C. Put in the frozen twists and cook for 10–12 minutes, flipping them over halfway through.

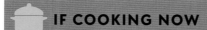 **IF COOKING NOW**

Follow the method in the 'making ahead to freeze' section up until the end of step 5.

OVEN

Preheat the oven to 180°C. Place the twists on a lined baking tray and cook for 18–20 minutes.

AIR FRYER

Preheat the air fryer to 180°C. Put in the twists and cook for 8–10 minutes, flipping them over halfway through.

GINGER SPICED OAT COOKIES

These ginger oat cookies are soft, chewy and everything you could want from a cookie. Find your jar of stem ginger in the home baking aisle. Have a bag of these made up in the freezer for those days when you just need something sweet!

Prep: 10 minutes | **Makes:** 8 large cookies

115g butter, at room temperature

1 cup (200g) light brown sugar

1 large egg

4 balls of stem ginger in syrup, drained and finely diced, plus 2 tsp of the syrup

1¼ cups (140g) plain flour

1 tsp ground ginger

1 tsp salt

½ tsp baking powder

¼ tsp bicarbonate of soda

¾ cup (80g) fine oats

❄ IF MAKING AHEAD TO FREEZE

1 Put the butter and sugar into a mixing bowl and mix with an electric whisk until light and fluffy.
2 Add the egg and stem ginger syrup and mix again.
3 Sift in the flour, ground ginger, salt, baking powder and bicarbonate of soda, and mix well. Fold through the oats and diced stem ginger.
4 Using an ice cream scoop, take out 8 scoops of the mix and roll them into balls.
5 Open a large labelled freezer bag. Keeping the bag flat, put in the cookie dough balls, leaving space so they don't stick together, then seal. Place flat in the freezer until fully frozen.

OVEN

Preheat the oven to 180°C. Put the frozen cookie dough balls on two large lined baking trays, giving them space to spread. Cook for 14–16 minutes, until golden, then remove from the oven and leave to sit for 20 minutes to firm up.

AIR FRYER

Preheat the air fryer to 170°C. Put the frozen cookie dough balls on baking parchment in the air fryer, giving them space to spread. Cook for 12–15 minutes, until golden, then remove and leave to sit for 20 minutes to firm up.

IF COOKING NOW

Follow the method in the 'making ahead to freeze' section up until the end of step 4.

OVEN

Preheat the oven to 180°C. Place the cookie dough balls on two large lined baking trays, giving them space to spread. Cook for 12–13 minutes, until golden, then remove from the oven and leave to sit for 20 minutes to firm up.

AIR FRYER

Preheat the air fryer to 170°C. Place the cookie dough balls on baking parchment in the air fryer, giving them space to spread. Cook for 10–11 minutes, until golden. Once cooked, remove and leave to sit for 20 minutes to firm up.

CHEESE & CHIVE SCONES

A good cheese scone is always a winner, and these are totally delicious. I always have a bag of these in the freezer and take out a couple to share if friends pop over.

Prep: 10 minutes | **Makes:** 6

2 cups (220g) self-raising flour

1 tsp baking powder

a pinch of salt

55g cold butter, cut into cubes

1 cup (140g) grated Cheddar

10g fresh chives, finely chopped

1 egg

½ cup (120ml) milk

1 tsp English mustard (optional)

To cook:
2 tbsp milk, for brushing

 IF MAKING AHEAD TO FREEZE

1 Put the flour, baking powder, salt and butter into a large mixing bowl and mix well, rubbing in the butter with your fingers until it looks like breadcrumbs. Stir in the grated cheese and the chopped chives.

2 In a small bowl, lightly beat together the egg, milk and mustard (if using). Pour into the dry mix and combine until it comes together in a rough dough.

3 Tip onto a work surface and bring together into a ball. Roll out the dough, using a rolling pin, to around 2cm deep.

4 Using an 8cm round cookie cutter, cut out 6 scones.

5 Open a large labelled freezer bag. Keeping the bag flat, put in the scones, leaving space so they don't stick together, and seal. Place flat in the freezer until fully frozen.

OVEN

Preheat the oven to 200°C. Place the frozen scones on a lined baking tray and brush with a little milk. Place in the oven for 17–20 minutes, until golden and risen.

AIR FRYER

Preheat the air fryer to 185°C. Brush the frozen scones with a little milk, then cook in the air fryer for 13–15 minutes, until golden and risen.

 IF COOKING NOW

Follow the method in the 'making ahead to freeze' section up until the end of step 4.

OVEN

Preheat the oven to 220°C. Place the scones on a lined baking tray and brush with a little milk. Place in the oven for 12–14 minutes, until golden and risen.

AIR FRYER

Preheat the air fryer to 190°C. Brush the scones with a little milk, then cook in the air fryer for 10–11 minutes, until golden and risen.

TIP

I like to serve these warm, with butter on top.

STUFFED CHOCOLATE CHIP COOKIES

These cookies are totally delicious. The oozing speculoos spread in the middle is such a wonderful surprise and will keep you coming back for more!

Prep: 15 minutes | **Makes:** 12

120g butter, at room temperature

¾ cup (150g) caster sugar

1 egg

1 tsp vanilla extract

1¾ cups (200g) plain flour

1 tsp baking powder

a pinch of salt

⅔ cup (100g) milk chocolate chips

⅔ cup (100g) white chocolate chips

12 tsp speculoos spread (I use Biscoff)

 ## IF MAKING AHEAD TO FREEZE

1 Put the butter and sugar into a mixing bowl and mix with an electric whisk until light and fluffy.
2 Add the egg and vanilla extract and mix again.
3 Sift in the flour, baking powder and salt. Add all the chocolate chips and mix together, using a spoon, to make a dough.
4 Place the cookie dough in the fridge for 30 minutes to firm up. Once firm, using an ice cream scoop, take out 12 scoops of the mix. Flatten each one with your finger and add 1 teaspoon of **speculoos spread** to each, then carefully close over and roll into a ball, making sure the filling is sealed.
5 Open a large labelled freezer bag. Keeping the bag flat, put in the cookie dough balls, leaving space so they don't stick together, and seal. Place flat in the freezer until fully frozen.

 ### OVEN

Preheat the oven to 180°C. Place the frozen cookie dough balls on two large lined baking trays, giving them space to spread. Cook for 14–16 minutes, until golden round the edges, then remove from the oven and leave to sit for 20 minutes to firm up.

 ### AIR FRYER

Preheat the air fryer to 170°C. Place the frozen cookie dough balls on baking parchment in the air fryer, giving them space to spread. Cook for 10–12 minutes, until golden round the edges, then remove and leave to sit for 20 minutes to firm up.

 ## IF COOKING NOW

Follow the method in the 'making ahead to freeze' section up until the end of step 4.

 ### OVEN

Preheat the oven to 180°C. Place the cookie dough balls on two large lined baking trays, giving them space to spread. Cook for 12–13 minutes, until golden round the edges, then remove from the oven and leave to sit for 20 minutes to firm up.

 ### AIR FRYER

Preheat the air fryer to 170°C. Place the cookie dough balls on baking parchment in the air fryer, giving them space to spread. Cook for 9–10 minutes, until golden round the edges, then remove and leave to sit for 20 minutes to firm up.

PRETZEL CORNFLAKE CRUNCH

This traybake is so easy to make. It's crunchy, salty and sweet, and tickles all the tastebuds! You only need a small amount of condensed milk – why not make another of my lovely traybakes to use up the rest of the tin?

Prep: 10 minutes | **Makes:** 16 slices

150g butter, at room temperature

½ cup plus 2 heaped tbsp (150ml) condensed milk

2 tbsp golden syrup

1 tsp vanilla extract

200g digestive biscuits

1 cup (50g) cornflakes

90g chocolate-covered pretzels, roughly chopped

 IF MAKING AHEAD TO FREEZE

1 Line a 20 x 20cm square tin with baking parchment.
2 Put the soft butter, condensed milk, golden syrup and vanilla extract into a mixing bowl and mix with an electric whisk until smooth.
3 Blitz the digestives in a food processor or put them into a freezer bag and bash it with a rolling pin until you have fine crumbs.
4 Add the biscuit crumbs to the bowl along with the cornflakes and chopped pretzels and combine into a dough.
5 Tip the dough into the lined tin, using the back of a spoon to press it in. Place in the fridge for 1 hour.
6 Remove the pretzel cornflake crunch from the fridge and cut it into 16 slices.
7 Put the slices into a large labelled freezer bag, seal and freeze flat.

READY TO EAT

Remove the traybake from the freezer and leave to defrost for 1 hour at room temperature. This is best kept in the fridge once defrosted.

 IF MAKING NOW

Follow the steps in the 'making ahead to freeze' section up until the end of step 6. It is now ready to eat. This will keep in the fridge for up to 5 days in an airtight container.

DARK CHOCOLATE FUDGE COOKIES

Gooey, chewy and seriously chocolaty, these cookies are to die for! Pick up the cute mini fudge chunks from the baking aisle in your local supermarket.

Prep: 10 minutes | **Makes:** 10

120g butter, at room temperature

1 cup (200g) light brown sugar

1 large egg

2 tsp vanilla extract

1 cup plus 1 heaped tbsp (125g) plain flour

⅓ cup (30g) cocoa powder

½ tsp salt

½ tsp baking powder

¼ tsp bicarbonate of soda

½ cup (80g) dark chocolate chips, plus a few extra to decorate

¼ cup (40g) mini fudge chunks

 ## IF MAKING AHEAD TO FREEZE

1 Put the butter and sugar into a mixing bowl and mix with an electric whisk until light and fluffy.
2 Add the egg and vanilla extract and mix again.
3 Sift in the flour, cocoa powder, salt, baking powder and bicarbonate of soda, and mix with a spoon until you have a dough. Fold in the chocolate chips and fudge chunks.

4 Using an ice cream scoop, take out 10 scoops of the mix and roll into balls. Gently press a few extra chocolate chips on top of each ball.
5 Open a large labelled freezer bag. Keeping the bag flat, put in the cookie dough balls, leaving space so they don't stick together, then seal. Place flat in the freezer until fully frozen.

OVEN

Preheat the oven to 180°C. Put the frozen cookie dough balls on two large lined baking trays, giving them space to spread. Cook for 12–14 minutes, then remove from the oven and leave to sit for 20 minutes to firm up.

AIR FRYER

Preheat the air fryer to 170°C. Put the frozen cookie dough balls on baking parchment in the air fryer. Cook for 9–10 minutes, then remove and leave to sit for 20 minutes to firm up.

 ## IF COOKING NOW

Follow the method in the 'making ahead to freeze' section up until the end of step 3. Now place the dough in the fridge for 30 minutes. When the dough has firmed up, using an ice cream scoop, scoop out 10 scoops of the mix and roll into balls. Gently press a few extra chocolate chips on top of each ball.

OVEN

Preheat the oven to 180°C. Place the cookie dough balls on two large lined baking trays, giving them space to spread. Cook for 12–13 minutes, then remove from the oven and leave to sit for 20 minutes to firm up.

AIR FRYER

Preheat the air fryer to 170°C. Place the cookie dough balls on baking parchment in the air fryer, giving them space to spread. Cook for 9–10 minutes, then remove and leave to sit for 20 minutes to firm up.

SHORTBREAD

Who doesn't love a buttery bit of shortbread? They are the perfect tea dunker or after-dinner treat! This is a great recipe to have in the freezer – simply break off as many rounds of shortbread as you want and cook.

Prep: 10 minutes | **Makes:** 20 small rounds

130g butter, at room temperature

½ cup (50g) caster sugar

1½ cups (165g) plain flour, plus extra for dusting

1 tsp vanilla extract

3 tbsp demerara sugar

 IF MAKING AHEAD TO FREEZE

1 Put the soft butter and caster sugar into a mixing bowl and mix together using an electric whisk until smooth.

2 Stir in the plain flour and vanilla extract using a spoon.

3 Once it comes together in a rough dough, tip the dough onto a lightly floured work surface and bring it together with your hands, then roll into a large sausage shape, evenly-sized throughout its length.

4 Sprinkle the demerara sugar on a chopping board and roll the sausage shape in the sugar to coat the outside.

5 Using a sharp knife, cut the shortbread sausage into 20 rounds.

6 Lightly push the rounds back together so you have a long sausage shape again, then wrap up well in cling film, put into a labelled freezer bag, seal and place in the freezer.

OVEN

Preheat the oven to 190°C. Unwrap and break off as many frozen shortbread rounds as you want. Place on a lined baking tray and cook for 17–20 minutes, until lightly golden.

AIR FRYER

Preheat the air fryer to 190°C. Unwrap and break off as many frozen shortbread rounds as you want and cook for 8–10 minutes, until lightly golden, flipping them over halfway through.

IF COOKING NOW

Follow the steps in the 'making ahead to freeze' method up until the end of step 5.

OVEN

Preheat the oven to 190°C. Place the shortbread rounds on a lined baking tray and cook for 15–16 minutes, until lightly golden.

AIR FRYER

Preheat the air fryer to 190°C. Put in the shortbread rounds and cook for 7–9 minutes, until lightly golden, flipping them over halfway through.

CHOCOLATE MALT SLICE

Who can resist a a chocolate slice! Perfect to have in the freezer for when the sweet craving strikes! These slices defrost in 1 hour, so are ideal for taking out in the morning, ready to take to work for a sweet treat.

Prep: 10 minutes | **Makes:** 16

300g plain digestive biscuits

¾ cup plus 2 heaped tbsp (200ml) condensed milk

200g chocolate spread (I use Nutella)

100g milk chocolate malt balls (I use Maltesers), lightly crushed

 IF MAKING AHEAD TO FREEZE

1 Line a 20 x 20cm square cake tin with baking parchment.
2 Blitz the digestives in a food processor or by putting them into a freezer bag and bashing with a rolling pin, until you have fine crumbs.
3 Add the digestives to a mixing bowl along with the condensed milk and the chocolate spread. Mix well.
4 Press into the lined tin, using the back of a spoon, and sprinkle over the lightly crushed **milk chocolate malt balls**. Lightly press them into the mix and place in the fridge for 1 hour to set.
5 Remove from the fridge and cut into 16 slices.
6 Put the slices into a large labelled freezer bag, seal and freeze flat.

READY TO EAT

Remove the traybake from the freezer and leave to defrost for 1 hour at room temperature. This is best kept in the fridge once defrosted.

IF MAKING NOW

Follow the method in the 'making ahead to freeze' section up until the end of step 5. It is now ready to eat. This will keep in the fridge for up to 5 days in an airtight container.

WHITE CHOCOLATE FUNFETTI COOKIES

These cookies are such fun, great to make with the kids and perfect for friends coming over or for kids' parties.

Prep: 10 minutes | **Makes:** 12

120g butter, at room temperature

1 cup (200g) caster sugar

1 egg

1 tsp vanilla extract

1⅔ cups (190g) plain flour

½ tsp baking powder

¼ tsp bicarbonate of soda

½ tsp salt

¼ cup (40g) rainbow sprinkles

170g white chocolate, cut into rough chunks

 ## IF MAKING AHEAD TO FREEZE

1 Put the butter and sugar into a mixing bowl and mix with an electric whisk until light and fluffy.
2 Add the egg and vanilla extract and mix again.
3 Sift in the flour, baking powder, bicarbonate of soda and salt and mix together using a spoon.
4 Fold in most of the sprinkles and the chopped white chocolate (reserving some to top the cookies).

5 Using an ice cream scoop, take out 12 scoops of the mix and roll into balls. I like to add a few sprinkles to the top of each ball, and a little chunk of white chocolate, pressing them on gently.
6 Open a large labelled freezer bag. Keeping the bag flat, put in the cookie dough balls, leaving space so they don't stick together, then seal. Place flat in the freezer until fully frozen.

 ### OVEN

Preheat the oven to 180°C. Put the frozen cookie dough balls on two large lined baking trays, giving them space to spread. Cook for 12–15 minutes, until golden round the edges, then remove from the oven and leave to sit for 20 minutes to firm up.

AIR FRYER

Preheat the air fryer to 170°C. Put the frozen cookie dough balls on baking parchment in the air fryer, giving them space to spread. Cook for 9–10 minutes, until golden round the edges, then remove and leave to sit for 20 minutes to firm up.

 ## IF COOKING NOW

1 Follow the method in the 'making ahead to freeze' section up until the end of step 4.
2 Place the cookie dough in the fridge for 30 minutes to firm up.

3 Using an ice cream scoop, take out 12 scoops of the mix and roll into balls. I like to add a few sprinkles to the top of each ball, and a little chunk of white chocolate, pressing them on gently.

 ### OVEN

Preheat the oven to 180°C. Put the cookie dough balls on two large lined baking trays, giving them space to spread. Cook for 12–15 minutes, until golden round the edges, then remove from the oven and leave to sit for 20 minutes to firm up.

AIR FRYER

Preheat the air fryer to 170°C. Put the cookie dough balls on baking parchment in the air fryer, giving them space to spread. Cook for 9–10 minutes, until golden round the edges, then remove and leave to sit for 20 minutes to firm up.

DESSERTS

HOT CHOCOLATE POTS

These hot chocolate pots are so decadent, and are totally delicious. Split them open and you get hot chocolate spread encased in sponge – so yummy. They are amazing to have in the freezer for when the sweet craving strikes. You will need four metal or ceramic ramekins.

Prep: 10 minutes　|　**Makes:** 4

140g butter, at room temperature, plus 1 tsp to grease the ramekins

scant ¾ cup (140g) caster sugar

2 eggs

1 tsp vanilla extract

1 cup (110g) plain flour

30g cocoa powder

4 heaped tsp chocolate spread (I use Nutella)

❄️ IF MAKING AHEAD TO FREEZE

1　Grease all four ramekins with the teaspoon of butter and set aside.
2　Put the butter and sugar into a mixing bowl and whisk until light and fluffy.
3　Add the eggs, vanilla, flour and cocoa powder, and whisk again until you have a lump-free batter.
4　Half-fill each ramekin with the batter.
5　Spoon 1 heaped teaspoon of chocolate spread into the centre of each ramekin, then cover with the rest of the batter.
6　Wrap each ramekin with cling film and tin foil, and place in the freezer.

🔲 OVEN

Preheat the oven to 160°C. Unwrap the ramekins and cook the frozen puddings for 25 minutes. Either run a knife carefully down the side of each and tip out onto a plate, or serve as they are in the ramekins.

🔲 AIR FRYER

Preheat the air fryer to 160°C. Unwrap the ramekins and cook the frozen puddings in the air fryer for 20 minutes. Either run a knife carefully down the side of each and tip out onto a plate, or serve as they are in the ramekins.

🍲 IF COOKING NOW

Follow the method in the 'making ahead to freeze' section up until the end of step 5.

🔲 OVEN

Preheat the oven to 160°C. Cook the puddings for 19 minutes. Either run a knife carefully down the side of each and tip out onto a plate, or serve as they are in the ramekins.

🔲 AIR FRYER

Preheat the air fryer to 160°C. Cook the puddings in the air fryer for 15 minutes. Either run a knife carefully down the side of each and tip out onto a plate, or serve as they are in the ramekins.

TIP
Serve with a dusting of icing sugar and some ice cream or double cream.

APPLE & CINNAMON TURNOVERS

These are such fun to make – why not get the kids involved? Crisp pastry with a lovely sweet apple filling – so delicious!

Prep: 10–15 minutes | **Makes:** 6

2 medium apples, peeled, cored and finely diced

3 tbsp caster sugar

juice of 1 lemon

2 tsp cornflour

1 tsp ground cinnamon

1 tsp vanilla extract

1 sheet of pre-rolled puff pastry

1 egg, beaten

demerara sugar, to sprinkle

 IF MAKING AHEAD TO FREEZE

1 Put the diced apples, caster sugar, lemon juice, cornflour, cinnamon and vanilla into a bowl and mix well.
2 Unroll the puff pastry and cut it into 6 equal squares.
3 Sharing it out between all 6, place the apple mix in the centre of each square, then fold one of the corners diagonally over the top of the filling to create a triangle shape.

4 Crimp the edge of each triangle with a fork, lightly pressing to seal the pastry.
5 Brush each turnover with beaten egg and sprinkle with demerara sugar.
6 Open a large labelled freezer bag. Keeping the bag flat, put in the turnovers, leaving space so they don't stick together, then seal. Place flat in the freezer until fully frozen.

OVEN

Preheat the oven to 180°C. Place the frozen turnovers on a lined baking tray and cook for 18–20 minutes, until golden.

AIR FRYER

Preheat the air fryer to 180°C. Cook the turnovers for 11–12 minutes, until golden, flipping them over halfway through.

IF COOKING NOW

Follow the method in the 'making ahead to freeze' section up until the end of step 5.

OVEN

Preheat the oven to 180°C. Place the turnovers on a lined baking tray and cook for 15 minutes, until golden.

AIR FRYER

Preheat the air fryer to 180°C. Cook the turnovers for 10 minutes, until golden, flipping them over halfway through.

TIP

Serve with a big dollop of ice cream or whipped cream.

BLUEBERRY CREAM CHEESE GALETTE

A perfect summer dessert to be enjoyed with friends – it's super easy to make and you can swap the blueberries for any other berries you might have!

Prep: 10 minutes | **Serves:** 6–8

1 cup plus 1 heaped tbsp (280g) cream cheese

3 heaped tbsp caster sugar

zest and juice of 1 lemon

250g fresh blueberries

1 tbsp cornflour

1 sheet of ready-rolled shortcrust pastry

1 egg, beaten

1 tbsp demerara sugar, to sprinkle

 ## ❄ IF MAKING AHEAD TO FREEZE

1 Put the cream cheese, 2 heaped tablespoons of caster sugar and the lemon zest into a bowl and mix well.
2 Put the blueberries into a separate bowl with the remaining heaped tablespoon of caster sugar, the lemon juice and the cornflour, and mix gently.
3 Unroll the shortcrust pastry rectangle, keeping it on its paper.
4 Spread the cream cheese mix on top, leaving a 5cm border round the edge.
5 Spoon the blueberries on top of the cream cheese.
6 Fold in the edges of the pastry, slightly overlapping – it does not need to be neat, it just needs to stop any filling leaking out the sides.
7 Brush the edges of the pastry with beaten egg and sprinkle with the demerara sugar.
8 Fold up the sides of the paper, then wrap well in cling film. Place it on a tray in the freezer and flash freeze for 2 hours, then put it into a large labelled freezer bag and seal.

 ### OVEN

Preheat the oven to 180°C. Remove the frozen galette from the freezer. Unwrap the cling film and place the galette on a lined baking tray. Cook for 45 minutes, until the crust is golden.

 ### AIR FRYER

Preheat the air fryer to 180°C. Unwrap the cling film and carefully slide the frozen galette into the air fryer, on its paper. Cook for 18–20 minutes, until golden. Cover with tin foil if it is browning too quickly.

 ## 🍲 IF COOKING NOW

Follow the method in the 'making ahead to freeze' section up until the end of step 7.

 ### OVEN

Preheat the oven to 180°C. Slide the galette onto a lined baking tray and cook for 30 minutes, until the crust is golden.

 ### AIR FRYER

Preheat the air fryer to 180°C. Slide the galette, still on its paper, into the air fryer and cook for 15–16 minutes, until golden, covering it with tin foil if it is browning too quickly.

TIP

Serve in slices, with some whipped cream or ice cream and a good dusting of icing sugar.

LEMON CURD & RASPBERRY SEMIFREDDO

This frozen dessert is so simple to whip up and is a real showstopper!
It is fruity and zesty and works brilliantly any time of year.

Prep: 10 minutes | **Serves:** 6–8

1 x 300ml tub of double cream

1 x 500g tub of Greek yoghurt

1 x 411g jar of lemon curd

150g fresh raspberries

zest of 1 lemon

6 meringues, roughly crushed

❄ IF MAKING AHEAD TO FREEZE

1 Line a 900g loaf tin with two or three layers of cling film big enough to hang over the sides of the tin.

2 Put the double cream into a mixing bowl and whisk with an electric whisk until just whipped, then add the yoghurt and lemon curd and whisk for another minute.

3 Lightly squish half the raspberries in a bowl, using a fork, and add to the creamy mix with the remaining whole raspberries and the lemon zest. Lightly fold through the crushed meringues.

4 Pour the mix into the lined loaf tin and cover with the overlapping cling film. Place in the freezer overnight.

READY TO EAT

Remove from the freezer and leave to sit for 5 minutes before unwrapping, slicing up and enjoying!

🍲 IF MAKING NOW

1 Follow the method in the 'making ahead to freeze' section to the end of step 4.

2 When ready to eat, remove from the freezer and leave to sit for 5 minutes before unwrapping and slicing up.

TIP
*Serve with extra
fresh raspberries.*

LIME & COCONUT CHEESECAKE

This no-bake cheesecake is epic. It's zesty and tropical and makes such a beautiful centrepiece. Decorate it however you like. I like to add extra lime zest and grated white chocolate to the top!

Prep: 15 minutes | **Serves:** 8

300g Hobnob biscuits

1 heaped tbsp butter, at room temperature

2 cups (500g) cream cheese

1 cup (240ml) double cream

½ cup (80g) icing sugar

zest and juice of 3 limes

3 heaped tbsp desiccated coconut

 IF MAKING AHEAD TO FREEZE

1   Blitz the Hobnobs in a food processor until you have fine crumbs. Add the butter, along with 1 heaped tablespoon of the cream cheese, and blitz again. The mix should come together nicely into a rough dough.

2   Squish the biscuit mix evenly into the base of a 20cm springform tin, using the back of a spoon to smooth it down. Place in the fridge while you make the filling.

3   Put the rest of the cream cheese, the double cream and icing sugar into a mixing bowl and beat with an electric whisk until lovely and thick. Stir through the zest and juice of the limes and the desiccated coconut.

4   Remove the base from the fridge and spoon the creamy mix on top, smoothing it as you go. Wrap well in cling film and place in the fridge for 2 hours to set.

5   Once set, make sure it is well covered by the cling film and slide into an extra large freezer bag before sealing and putting it into the freezer.

READY TO EAT

Remove from the freezer and leave to fully defrost, then unwrap, slice up and serve.

 IF MAKING NOW

Follow the method in the 'making ahead to freeze' section up until the end of step 4. Once the cheesecake is set, unwrap, slice up and serve.

VEGAN COOKIE DOUGH SKILLET

Warm cookie dough is such a crowd-pleaser, I promise this will go down so well with everyone whether they are vegan or not! This is serious chocolate decadence – you have to give it a go!

Prep: 10 minutes | **Serves:** 6–8

½ cup (100g) soft brown sugar

⅓ cup (70g) caster sugar

1¾ cups (200g) plain flour

1½ tsp baking powder

⅓ cup plus 1 tsp (80g) coconut oil, at room temperature

1 tsp vanilla extract

¼ cup plus 1 tbsp (70ml) oat milk

200g vegan dark chocolate, cut into chunks

 IF MAKING AHEAD TO FREEZE

1   Put the soft brown sugar, caster sugar, flour and baking powder into a bowl and mix with a spoon.
2   Add the coconut oil, vanilla extract, oat milk and chocolate pieces and mix until it comes together in a dough.
3   Put the dough into a labelled freezer bag and squish flat before freezing.

 OVEN

Remove from the freezer and leave to defrost. Preheat the oven to 180°C. Squish the cookie dough into a pie dish or skillet approx. 22cm in size and place in the oven for 25 minutes. It should still be soft in the middle but golden round the outside.

 AIR FRYER

Remove from the freezer and leave to defrost. Preheat the air fryer to 180°C. Squish the cookie dough into an air fryer-safe dish and cook in the air fryer for 13–15 minutes, covering with tin foil if needed. It should still be soft in the middle but golden round the outside.

 IF COOKING NOW

Follow the method in the 'making ahead to freeze' section up until the end of step 2.

 OVEN

Preheat the oven to 180°C. Squish the cookie dough into a pie dish or skillet approx. 22cm in size and place in the oven for 25 minutes. It should still be soft in the middle but golden round the outside.

 AIR FRYER

Preheat the air fryer to 180°C. Squish the cookie dough into an air fryer-safe dish and cook in the air fryer for 13–15 minutes, covering with tin foil if browning too quickly. It should still be soft in the middle but golden round the outside.

TIP
Serve with a few scoops of vegan coconut ice cream.

CARAMEL LAVA PUDDINGS

These caramel puddings with an oozy middle are sensational. Add a big dollop of ice cream or a generous pouring of double cream for even more decadence. You will need four metal or ceramic ramekins.

Prep: 10 minutes | **Makes:** 4

140g butter, at room temperature, plus 1 extra tsp to grease the ramekins

scant ¾ cup (140g) light brown sugar

2 eggs

1 tsp vanilla extract

1 cup plus 1 heaped tbsp (140g) plain flour

4 heaped tsp tinned caramel

 ## IF MAKING AHEAD TO FREEZE

1 Grease all four ramekins with the teaspoon of butter and set aside.
2 Put the butter and sugar into a mixing bowl and whisk until light and fluffy.
3 Add the eggs, vanilla extract and flour and whisk again until you have a lump-free batter.
4 Half-fill each ramekin with the batter.
5 Spoon 1 heaped teaspoon of the caramel into the centre of each ramekin, then cover with the rest of the batter.
6 Wrap each ramekin with cling film and tin foil and place in the freezer.

 ### OVEN

Preheat the oven to 160°C. Unwrap the ramekins and cook the frozen puddings for 25 minutes. Either run a knife carefully down the side of each pudding and tip out onto a plate or serve as they are in their ramekins.

 ### AIR FRYER

Preheat the air fryer to 160°C. Unwrap the ramekins and cook the frozen puddings in the air fryer for 20 minutes. Either run a knife carefully down the side of each and tip out onto a plate, or serve as they are in the ramekins.

 ## IF COOKING NOW

Follow the method in the 'making ahead to freeze' up until the end of step 5.

 ### OVEN

Preheat the oven to 160°C. Cook the puddings for 20 minutes. Either run a knife carefully down the side of each and tip out onto a plate, or serve as they are in the ramekins.

 ### AIR FRYER

Preheat the air fryer to 160°C. Cook the puddings in the air fryer for 16 minutes. Either run a knife carefully down the side of each and tip out onto a plate, or serve as they are in the ramekins.

TIP
Dust with icing sugar and serve with ice cream or double cream.

RASPBERRY & ELDERFLOWER SORBET

This light and refreshing sorbet is such a delicious way to finish a meal. It is so easy to make, and it's great to have in the freezer for when you need something sweet.

Prep: 10 minutes | **Serves:** 4

500g fresh raspberries

juice of 1 lemon

¾ cup (180ml) elderflower cordial

 IF MAKING AHEAD TO FREEZE

1 Put the raspberries into a blender with the lemon juice and give them a blitz. Pour through a sieve, using the back of a spoon to scrape the blended berries through as much as you can, leaving the seeds behind to discard.

2 Put the berry pulp back into the blender along with the cordial and mix again.

3 Once combined, pour the mix into a container with a lid.

4 Place in the freezer and leave to freeze overnight, until firm.

READY TO EAT

Remove from the freezer and leave it to sit for 10 minutes before serving.

 IF MAKING NOW

1 Follow the method in the 'making ahead to freeze' section to the end of step 4.

2 When ready to eat, remove from the freezer and leave it to sit for 10 minutes before serving.

BANOFFEE FILO CUPS

All the flavours of a banoffee pie encased in crispy filo pastry –
so delicious! Put them straight into the oven from frozen and
you've got a delicious dessert in no time.

Prep: 10–15 minutes | **Makes:** 8

4–5 tbsp vegetable oil

4 large sheets of filo pastry

1 x 397g tin of caramel

2 bananas, peeled and sliced

 IF MAKING AHEAD TO FREEZE

1 Lightly oil 8 holes of a muffin tin, using a brush.

2 Lay the 4 pastry sheets on top of each other on a work surface and cut into 8 squares.

3 Take one filo pile and remove the top three layers. Brush the bottom square with a little oil, then place another square on top but on an angle. Brush with oil again and do this a third time. You should have one square left.

4 Push the little stack of pastry into a muffin tin hole and spoon in 1 heaped teaspoon of caramel. Layer on 2–3 slices of banana, and finish with another teaspoon of caramel, making sure to cover all the banana. Add the final square of filo on top of the caramel, then brush all over with oil and gently fold the edges in. Repeat with the rest of the filo stacks.

5 Wrap the muffin tin tray with cling film and place in the freezer. After 2 hours, you can remove the cups and place them carefully in a freezer bag, then seal, and put back into the freezer to save space.

 OVEN

Preheat the oven to 180°C. Place the frozen cups on a baking tray and cook for 14–15 minutes, until golden.

AIR FRYER

Preheat the air fryer to 180°C. Place the frozen cups in an air fryer-safe dish, and cook carefully for 7–8 minutes, until golden.

 IF COOKING NOW

Follow the method in the 'making ahead to freeze' section up until the end of step 4.

 OVEN

Preheat the oven to 180°C. Place the full muffin tin in the oven and cook for 12–14 minutes, until golden.

AIR FRYER

Preheat the air fryer to 180°C. Place the full muffin tin in the air fryer. If your tin will not fit, carefully remove the cups from the muffin tin and place in an air fryer-safe dish, making sure they are packed in together to keep them from spreading. Cook for 5–6 minutes, until golden.

TIP
Serve warm, with ice cream!

FROZEN CUSTARD

This is a mix between ice cream and custard, lovely scooped on top of a hot chocolate dessert or a sticky toffee pudding. Perfect for when you want custard and ice cream and can't decide which!

Prep: 5 minutes | **Serves:** 8

1¼ cups (300ml) double cream

1 x 397g tin of condensed milk

1 tbsp custard powder

1¼ cups (300ml) ready-made custard

 IF MAKING AHEAD TO FREEZE

1 Put the double cream, condensed milk and custard powder into a mixing bowl and beat with an electric whisk for 3–4 minutes, until it starts to thicken.

2 Mix in the custard with a spatula until it all comes together, then pour into a tub with a lid and freeze overnight.

READY TO EAT

Remove from the freezer and leave to sit for 10 minutes before serving.

 IF MAKING NOW

1 Follow the method in the 'making ahead to freeze' section up until the end of step 2.

2 When ready to eat, remove from the freezer and leave to sit for 10 minutes before serving.

TIP
Serve on top of hot desserts or just as it is!

MANAGING YOUR FREEZER

How to get started

Give your freezer a good clear-out. Be ruthless – get rid of anything you know you won't eat or anything that is badly freezer burnt. Store what you want to keep in a cool bag in a cold dark area until you have cleaned and defrosted your freezer; if you work quickly, it will be back in the freezer in a few hours. Once it's defrosted and switched back on, you can refill it, listing everything you have. A magnetic freezer list attached to the freezer is a simple way to do this – simply score off anything you take out, and then when you add something to the freezer, be sure to add it to the list too.

Organising your freezer

THREE-DRAWER FREEZER
Freezers work more efficiently and use less energy if they are full, so a three-drawer freezer can be perfect for all your needs.

- Keep one drawer for your Grab and Cook meals, with space on the top for your flash freezing tray.

- Use one drawer for products such as ice creams, ice lollies, fish fingers, etc. In order to get maximum use out of the space, decant food from supermarket boxes and store it in freezer bags. Supermarkets love to make products feel larger by packaging them in a box, but often a lot of the content is air.

- Your third drawer is great for all your ready-frozen ingredients such as herbs and vegetables, frozen fruit, etc.

CHEST FREEZER
A chest freezer can hold a lot of food, and means you always have food to hand and can enjoy the cost savings of buying in bulk. The downside is they are often just one large space that can be hard to keep organised. My top tip is to use large plastic boxes or baskets to divide up the space – one box for meat, one for vegetables, one for your collection of Grab and Cook meals, etc. Having a well-organised freezer will make it easier to use and keep it helping you.

ROTATING THE FOOD IN YOUR FREEZER
Remember, the object of being organised is that the meals are being used and rotated, not just stored. As you add new meals to your freezer, it's a good idea to put them at the back and move the older things to the front – that way you keep a good rotation of food and nothing has time to get freezer burn.

FREEZER BURN
Freezer burn occurs when food has been damaged by dehydration due to air reaching the food. It is generally caused by food not being securely wrapped in airtight packaging. It is not dangerous to eat food that is freezer burnt, though the product or meal may be drier and not taste as good. Always store food in freezer bags, squeezing out as much air as possible as you seal the bag up, and always try to use the food following the guideline dates.

KEEPING YOUR FREEZER AT THE CORRECT TEMPERATURE
The recommended temperature your freezer should be set at is -18°C/0°F, but your freezer may have to be set slightly higher or lower depending on the temperature of the area where it is located. Freezers do not work well when placed in areas of extreme temperatures – if your freezer is placed in an uninsulated cold garage or shed, be careful in the winter months, as it can shut down if the outside temperature drops below freezing. Slightly heating the space with a small heater in extreme winter months can help combat this.

How to defrost and clean your freezer

Many modern freezers have a defrost button. If your freezer has one of these, refer to the manufacturer's guidelines on how to proceed. If you don't have a defrost button, follow these steps:

- **STEP 1:** Turn off your freezer and remove all food, storing it in coolers, or in the fridge, until the process is complete.

- **STEP 2:** Lay out towels, trays or plastic to collect the water; you can also place old towels on the bottom shelves to help absorb excess moisture. If your freezer has a drainage hose, make sure the end is in a bucket, so that all the water is collected.

- **STEP 3:** Let the ice melt. This is best done naturally with the door open; however, if you want to speed up the process, you can place a bowl of warm water on a towel on a freezer shelf. Use plastic spatulas to help remove some of the ice, being careful not to damage the appliance.

- **STEP 4:** Once all the ice has melted and the excess towels and water are cleared away, give the inside of the freezer a quick clean with 1 tablespoon of bicarbonate of soda to 4 cups (960ml) of hot water. Clean with a cloth and wipe dry before turning on the freezer again.

- **STEP 5:** Once your freezer gets down to temperature, you can start to put everything back in. This is a good time to do a quick inventory and organise it.

CHECK THE SEAL

It's always a good idea to check your freezer seal. Having a strong seal will help your freezer maintain the correct temperature. Sometimes seals can get dusty or mouldy, but regular cleaning should help keep the seal tight.

What to do in a power cut

None of us want to see our meals wasted when a long power cut occurs, so follow the simple rules below to help save your freezer food.

- The most important thing to remember is to keep the door closed, so don't open the freezer to check it.

- A full freezer will keep its temperature for about 48 hours or more. A half-filled freezer will last for about 24 hours, so the fuller the freezer the longer the food will stay frozen.

- When organising your freezer, remember that it will defrost from the top down, so store large cuts of meats or expensive items at the bottom, with cheaper bread products, etc. at the top.

- Once the power returns, open the freezer to check what food has defrosted. You can't refreeze defrosted food, unless you cook it first. So you should throw away anything you are unsure of, especially poultry and seafood. If red meat has defrosted and is still cold, you can cook it and refreeze it once cooked. But if in doubt, be safe and bin it!

ORGANISED KITCHENS

The kitchen is often the hardest place to keep neat, tidy and clean. Every family member uses the space and it is often the dumping ground for the whole family, the initial repository for every item that enters the house. Our kitchen is not just used for cooking – it's also a storage area, a homework area, a laundry area . . . no wonder it's a hard space to keep organised!

Fear not, for those of you who have seen my kitchen on social media or TV will know I am ruthless. There shall be no dumping of anyone's things in my kitchen . . . if it doesn't belong in the kitchen it's not staying there. My kitchen not only has to be a place to cook and eat and a place for the family to hang out and catch up, it's also my workspace. It's where I test my recipes and film my social media content, so it's got to work well as a space. Over the years, I've accumulated tips and tricks to keep it tidy and clean, and I'm going to share them below – I hope they help you too.

SOMEONE SHOULD OWN THE SPACE

Whoever is the main cook in the house should try to be the owner of the space – that way one person can rule over the area and see to it that it's not a communal dumping ground. This is not to say that it's the responsibility of just that one person to cook in it and clean it – it certainly isn't!

START WITH A CLEAR-OUT, BIG OR SMALL

It's hard to cook in a room that's full and messy, and not just physically hard, it's mentally hard too. Having a clean, well-ordered kitchen will automatically help you in the process of prepping meals, cooking and baking. If you find it too overwhelming to think about cleaning and tidying the whole kitchen, start small. Clean out one cupboard or drawer each day for a week and see how much you've achieved by the end of those seven days.

WHERE TO KEEP THINGS

As you clear out and declutter, whatever's left is what you generally need to get the jobs done. As you put things away, try to store them as you will need them – so if you use something every day, keep it at the front of the cupboard, and store items you don't use so much at the back. Keep all the main gadgets that you use every day out on the counter (if you have space), such as the toaster, kettle, coffee machine, smoothie maker, etc. That way you free up more cupboard space.

MAXIMISE YOUR SPACE

If you want to maximise your cupboard and drawer space, have a think about where else in the kitchen you can store things. For example, all my herbs and spices are on two large racks screwed to the back of a cupboard door. It's easy to spot which ones are running low, and it keeps them neat and tidy and frees up the cupboard for more storage. Pots and pans are great kept in a pot rack on an empty bit of wall, or can be hung from the ceiling. If you have nice wooden chopping boards, these can be hung up on display too. I have large round pizza chopping boards in place of a picture on my kitchen wall, and they look great! Finally, use all the space in your kitchen cupboards, not just the shelves – use the walls of the cupboards too. I attach small screws, then use the redundant area for hanging things like measuring spoons, kitchen scissors, sieves, etc.

BUY SPACE-SAVING NESTING PRODUCTS

If you re-buy anything for the kitchen, space-efficient, stacking products will really help save on space and clutter. By this I mean bowls and pots that fit inside one another, stacking Tupperware, space-saving knife racks, etc. Even if you have a very large kitchen, stacking products really help keep everything neat and tidy.

DON'T DECANT EVERYTHING INTO JARS

It's easy to get sucked in by Instagram – pictures of beautifully decanted dry ingredients all in the same-

sized jars, perfectly labelled and lined up. However, we all know that hidden somewhere else there must be partially-full packets containing the rest of the food that wouldn't fit into the jar. The jar also has no nutritional info or use-by date on it. Stick to the original packets, unless you really want a few out on display. If you do want to organise your ingredients, I suggest getting a few baskets or boxes where you can keep similar products stored together.

GET A LARGE JUNK BOWL

My top tip, and something I use every day! Anything left lying around – pens, screwdrivers, batteries, hair clips, Sellotape, etc. that doesn't belong in the kitchen – add it to the bowl. Once a week, or even once a fortnight, dump it out on the kitchen table and make everyone grab what's theirs before putting the rest in its proper place or in the bin. Believe me, I've done this for years and it's amazing what ends up in the kitchen junk bowl. I always sift any money out before I shout at the rest of the family to claim their belongings – my charge for lifting the misplaced items into the bowl in the first place, and a useful lesson for my kids!

CLEAR THE DECKS

Try to keep counters and tables as clear as possible. People are less likely to make a mess or leave junk lying around if the counters are clear. Clear work surfaces also help you maintain good kitchen hygiene and give you space to do what needs to be done in that area. I'm a huge fan of a kitchen table, if you can fit one in. Nowadays, you can get fab space-saving tables that are attached to the wall. None of the recipes in the book are cooked before going into the freezer, so remember you can simply sit at the kitchen table and make them up.

LAY OUT THE KITCHEN FOR YOUR NEEDS

Got kids? Try to put plates, bowls, cups and kids' cutlery at kid-friendly height – that way they can set the table or fend for themselves without having to always ask for your help. See pages 244 and 245 for more info on kids in the kitchen.

RAISING CAPABLE KIDS IN THE KITCHEN

We all want to raise our children to be capable adults, but sometimes the actual practicalities can be tough. Life can be busy, and it's sometimes easier to do the job yourself, particularly with teaching them how to cook, because there are so many different things you have to factor in.

The kitchen can be a dangerous place for little ones – there are hot things, sharp things, and small kids often need to stand on a chair or a stool to reach the countertop, thus adding another hazard into the mix. My Grab and Cook recipes can be made sitting at the kitchen table, well away from any hot cooking hazards, making them very simple to teach.

When I started *The Batch Lady*, my goal was to show people that you can cook when you want to, eat when you want to. Preparing and cooking are two separate tasks that do not need to be completed at the same time. When teaching children how to cook, we can split cooking into these two phases, not moving on to cooking until the first phase is mastered and the child is old enough. In that way, you are able to halve the amount that you need to teach, allowing small children to learn to love making meals (and enjoy the satisfaction of helping to prepare meals) without any of the danger of being around a hot appliance.

On page 246, I have listed the recipes that I think will be great to start children batching. Choose a few simple ones, lay the ingredients on the table and show them how to make their own meals. It's safe, simple and very rewarding! Using the Grab and Cook method can be great fun for kids – it's quick, easy and has few rules, so they can have a good time and be rewarded with the yummy treat they've made while you relax in the knowledge that you have taught them a skill that will help them immensely in life.

DEALING WITH FUSSY EATERS
If you have a fussy eater, why not get them to choose a recipe that they think sounds good from page 246?

If there's an ingredient that they don't like in the recipe, give them a few suggestions for different things they could use instead. That way your fussy eater feels in control of their own food, having made it themselves to their exact requirements.

WHAT AGE CAN I START BATCHING WITH KIDS?

- **2–5 years**
  Kids as young as two can begin batching, so get them started on mixing, measuring out the ingredients using measuring spoons, and putting all the ingredients into the freezer bags. It's a good idea to double the amount, so you can show the younger children how to do it and they follow your lead.

- **5–10 years**
  From when they are around five, you can start to get kids chopping, and there are some great kids' knife sets on the market that allow your child to chop safely. Once your child has mastered chopping, there are many recipes that they can start to make. By the age of ten, they could make every recipe in this book – because remember, we are only talking about stage one, which is preparing the recipe for the freezer, not actually cooking it.

This is a great age to start to teach food safety. A good way of doing this is to use a recipe such as stuffed chicken breasts, so you can show them how they must wash the knife and use a different chopping board for different ingredients.

- **10 years and above**

  If you've completed stage one with your children, you can move on to stage two, so that they can not only prepare meals for the freezer but can now cook them. Try to start stage two with easy recipes that perhaps just need to be placed on a tray, like the fish parcels on page 130, or a Grab and Cook bag that simply needs to be poured into a slow cooker.

AIR FRYERS AND PRESSURE COOKERS

Some appliances are better than others when it comes to teaching children. Air fryers and pressure cookers have various extra elements of danger compared to other methods, therefore I recommend teaching kids how to cook food in an oven, microwave or slow cooker first, moving on to air fryer cooking in their teens and leaving pressure cooking until adulthood.

SCHOOL HOLIDAYS

School holidays are a perfect time to get kids batching – it's a practical use of their time and it's a fun thing to do. Through the summer holidays, you could have one morning a week when you all sit around the table batching meals. Perhaps you can add the name of the child who batched that specific meal to the bag or container before putting it into the freezer, so you can give them a shout out on the night you cook it. This sense of achievement and pride will encourage your child to want to batch more often. Teaching children young will make your life so much easier when they are teenagers – imagine being able to phone home and ask your teen to take a meal out of the freezer and cook it, ready for when you arrive home. When your kids leave home, you will have given them amazing skills that many other children could only dream of.

Hand washing

It's brilliant to think that children have made the meals you will eat as a family, but remember, you want these meals to be prepared in the best conditions. Here is a hand washing guide to teach your child before starting phase one, to keep everyone safe and healthy.

1 Turn on the tap.

2 Wash your hands with water.

3 Apply one or two squirts of hand soap.

4 Rub your hands together.

5 Wash all the soap off of your hands.

6 Use a towel or elbow to turn off the tap.

7 Dry your hands.

Recipes suitable for kids to make

MEAL PLANNING

Planning what you are going to eat in the week ahead can really help your headspace. I suggest planning 3–5 days only, allowing you some wiggle room and a day to use up leftovers. Each Grab and Cook recipe takes on average 5–10 minutes to make, which really helps you get organised and in control not only of your meals, but of your food shopping and budget.

MAIN EVENING MEALS

Evening meals are the most important to organise, as they are often more complicated than breakfast and lunch, and are, of course, needed at the most tiresome and busy time of the day. If you're just getting started, it's a good idea to simply plan your dinners for the week ahead – then once you are up and running, you can start to do the same for lunches and breakfasts.

Most of us generally eat the same 8–10 dinners on a rotational basis. If you find recipes that you and the family like, double them up when you make them so you always have one for that night and one for the freezer. Having a bank of meals in the freezer will help you on a busy week when you have no time to cook, or when you are perhaps tight for cash before payday.

LUNCHES

I'm always being asked for more lunch options, and there are lots in this book to choose from. I would suggest taking a lunch option out of the freezer the night before you need it and cooking it at the same time as dinner; that way it can be taken cold in packed lunches or heated in the microwave at work. By cooking tomorrow's lunch at the same time as today's dinner, you will save on using electricity or gas, and you will save hugely on cost, as taking a lunch from home is considerably cheaper than eating lunch out. If you find that you are spending a lot of money on lunches, having a few days a week when you get organised and take lunch from home will really help.

PLANNING A WHOLE WEEK?

Don't know where to start? Don't worry, I have you covered – why not try following my five meals in 30 minutes on page 249? This section gives you a variety of five midweek meals, the shopping list, and a step-by-step guide to getting them made and put into the freezer. Once you have mastered these five, why not choose five different recipes from my Weeknight section and give it a go for another week?

Making a plan for dinner

Below are some weekly meal plans for dinner for 5 weeks, to give you some inspiration and help you get started. All the dinners in this list are in the book, and they all take just 5–15 minutes to prepare for the freezer. Choose a week you like the look of and start getting those meals into your freezer, ready for the busy weeks ahead. If planning 5 days seems overwhelming, you can start with 2 or 3 nights each week.

WEEK 1	1. Romano stuffed peppers 2. Creamy sausage & cannellini bean one-pot 3. Goat's cheese & sun-dried tomato stuffed chicken breasts 4. Bombay fish fingers 5. Honey sesame chicken
WEEK 2	1. Salmon & noodle parcels 2. Spinach, pea & mint pasta 3. Crunchy tomato, cod & pea parcels 4. Satay chicken curry 5. Tex Mex burger
WEEK 3	1. Soy chilli beef & peppers 2. Baked honey & mustard pork chops 3. Chicken shawarma traybake 4. Romesco pasta 5. Currywurst
WEEK 4	1. Coconut, spinach & tomato dhal 2. Pizza-stuffed chicken breasts 3. Minted lamb burgers 4. Beef olives 5. Pork carnitas
WEEK 5	1. Mediterranean gnocchi pesto bake 2. Beef ragù 3. Jerk-spiced hake parcels 4. Creamy sausage & cannellini bean one-pot 5. Slow-cooked Korean-style beef

5–15 MINS

Let's make five meals in 30 minutes

Want to get organised for the week ahead in 30 minutes? I've given you five fast recipes from the Weeknight chapter, so simply follow the steps below and in 30 minutes you will have five meals bagged up and in the freezer, ready to grab and cook whenever you need them.

THE MEALS YOU WILL MAKE IN THIS FAST SECTION ARE:

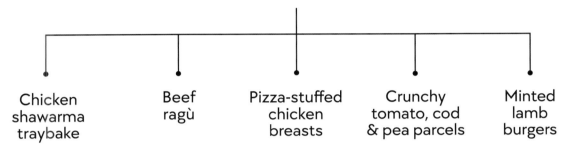

| Chicken shawarma traybake | Beef ragù | Pizza-stuffed chicken breasts | Crunchy tomato, cod & pea parcels | Minted lamb burgers |

THE SHOPPING LIST
Go through your cupboards, fridge and freezer at home and mark off anything you already have, then you will know what you need to buy when you go shopping.

Fresh fruit, veg and herbs
· 1 lemon
· 2 red peppers
· 3 red onions
· 1 large carrot
· 2 celery sticks
· 2 cloves of garlic
· a bunch of fresh basil

Dairy
· 1 x 240g ball of mozzarella
· 47g grated Cheddar

Frozen
· 300g frozen sweet potato chunks

· 115g frozen diced onions
· frozen chopped garlic
· 280g frozen peas

Storecupboard
· ground coriander
· ground cumin
· paprika
· dried mint
· bay leaves
· tomato purée
· 1 beef stock cube
· 2 cups (500ml) passata
· 4 tbsp shop-bought pizza sauce
· 4 tbsp sun-dried tomato pesto

· 8 tbsp panko breadcrumbs
· olive oil
· salt
· black pepper

Meat/fish
· 6–8 skinless and boneless chicken thighs
· 4 chicken breasts
· 750g diced stewing beef
· 12 slices of pepperoni
· 4 cod fillets
· 500g lamb mince

Alcohol
· ½ cup (120ml) red wine

Lay out all the ingredients, a pile for each recipe. Then just begin the first recipe and follow the directions – each recipe should take only 5 or 6 minutes to prep.

Chicken shawarma traybake

2 cloves of garlic, grated
1 tbsp ground coriander
1 tsp ground cumin
2 tsp paprika
juice of 1 lemon
4 tbsp olive oil
1 tsp salt
6–8 skinless and boneless chicken thighs
2 red peppers, deseeded and cut into thick strips
2 red onions, cut into thick chunks
300g frozen sweet potato chunks

1   Combine the grated garlic, the coriander, cumin, smoked paprika, lemon juice, olive oil and salt in a large bowl and mix into a paste.

2   Add the chicken thighs, red peppers, red onions and sweet potato chunks and give everything a good mix.

3   Put into a large labelled freezer bag and freeze flat.

Beef ragù

1 cup (115g) frozen diced onions
2 tsp frozen chopped garlic
1 large carrot, peeled and finely diced
2 celery sticks, finely diced
2 tbsp tomato purée
2 bay leaves
1 beef stock cube, crumbled
salt and pepper
2 cups (500ml) passata
½ cup (120ml) red wine
750g diced stewing beef

1   Put everything apart from the stewing beef into a large labelled freezer bag and mix together.

2   Put the diced beef into a separate freezer bag and slot inside the larger freezer bag, then seal and freeze flat.

Pizza-stuffed chicken breasts

4 skinless and boneless chicken breasts
4 tbsp shop-bought pizza sauce
1 x 240g ball of mozzarella, drained and cut into 8 slices
12 slices of pepperoni
a handful of fresh basil
2 tsp paprika
2 tbsp olive oil

1   On a chopping board, cut down the side of each chicken breast to create a pocket, making sure you don't cut all the way through.

2   Open the pocket and add 1 tablespoon of pizza sauce, 2 slices of mozzarella, 3 slices of pepperoni and a few basil leaves. Close the pocket. Repeat with the rest of the chicken breasts.

3   Put the paprika and olive oil into a shallow bowl and stir, then brush the oil over each chicken breast.

4   Put the chicken into a large labelled freezer bag. Freeze flat.

Crunchy tomato, cod & pea parcels

2 cups (280g) frozen peas
4 cod fillets
4 tbsp sun-dried tomato pesto
8 tbsp panko breadcrumbs
1/3 cup (47g) grated Cheddar

1 Cut 4 squares of tin foil 35 x 30cm.

2 Divide the frozen peas between the tin foil squares, placing them in a pile in the centre of each one.

3 Place the cod fillets on top of the peas and spread each one with 1 tablespoon of pesto.

4 Mix the breadcrumbs and grated cheese in a small bowl, and distribute this breadcrumb mixture on top of the cod fillets – the pesto helps the breadcrumbs stick. Wrap each parcel up.

5 Put the wrapped parcels into a large labelled freezer bag and freeze flat.

Minted lamb burgers

500g lamb mince
1 red onion, finely diced
1 tsp frozen chopped garlic
1 tbsp dried mint
1 tsp salt
a good grind of black pepper

1 Put all the ingredients into a large bowl and mix together with your hands.

2 Tip the mix onto a work surface and divide in half. Split each half into 4 to give you 8 equal-sized pieces. Roll each piece into a ball, then press down to form a burger shape.

3 Open your large labelled freezer bag. Keeping the bag flat, put in the burgers, leaving space so they don't stick together. If stacking them on top of each other, add a layer of baking parchment to stop them sticking. Freeze flat.

Congratulations!

You have made five nights' worth of dinners in 30 minutes. The five labelled bags are in your freezer, ready to grab and cook whenever you need them. They will keep for 90 days in the freezer. When you want to use them, simply refer back to the recipe in the Weeknight chapter (see page 90), to choose your method of cooking.

INDEX

THANKS

Grab and Cook has been such a fun book to create and I want to use this page to virtually grab, hug and thank all the amazing people who have made it possible to take this book from a vision in my head to an actual book on the shelves.

This is my first book published by Ebury, Penguin. It's been lovely joining a new team, and what a fantastic bunch of people they are. A huge thank you to Lizzy Gray (Deputy Publisher), who believed in me from the first time we met, instantly got my vision and continued to guide me through each stage of the book. To my wonderful editor Emily Brickell, who is so organised and efficient and makes everything work seamlessly, thank you. It's been great getting to know you and bringing this book so easily to its final stages. A huge thanks also to Lucy Harrison (Senior Production Manager), Abby Watson (Head of Campaigns) and the rest of the team at Ebury.

My vision for this book was to allow the reader to make their own decisions as they go through: Make for now or for the freezer? Cook in a slow cooker or in an air fryer? These ideas are always fun but getting them to fit on a page, look good and remain simple to follow can be a lot tougher. Therefore a huge thanks deservedly goes to the designer Nikki Dupin at Studio Nic&Lou, for making this happen and for creating the front cover too. Another thanks to copy editor Annie Lee for making sure that every detail in the book is correct.

The wonderful photography in this book is thanks to Andrew Hayes-Watkins and the fab team Lola Milne (Food Stylist) and Rachel Vere (Prop Stylist). What a fun few weeks we had shooting this book! I'm usually very nervous on photoshoots but Andrew, you made it such fun, with your show-and-tells and would-you-rather questions, I can't wait to see what pops out of your car boot the next time we work together!

To my agent Cathryn Summerhayes at Curtis Brown, it has been a big year full of changes and with exciting times ahead. Thank you for all the guidance, advice and wisdom that you give me. You've been there since the very start of my journey with The Batch Lady and I appreciate you always being there for me.

Now to my team of one, Nicola Bruce, who continues to work by my side every day, I so appreciate you and all that you do – doing this on my own would be lonely and no fun, working with you makes it perfect. Thank you for your years of hard work and dedication. You continue to grow every year and never seem to flinch when I continuously throw new project ideas at you... which I do a lot, and often before we have finished the last exciting idea... sorry!

And last but never least, a huge thank you to my husband, Peter, and my children, Jake and Zara. Peter, you are my rock and my soulmate, and I am so lucky to get to go through life with you by my side. Jake and Zara, thank you for being my ever-fearless taste testers! In the five years since I started The Batch Lady you have grown up so much, I am so proud of who you are and who you are growing into. You are my greatest achievements. Thank you for always believing in me too.

1

Ebury Press, an imprint of Ebury Publishing
20 Vauxhall Bridge Road
London SW1V 2SA

Ebury Press is part of the Penguin Random House group of companies whose addresses
can be found at global.penguinrandomhouse.com

First published by Ebury Press in 2024

www.penguin.co.uk

A CIP catalogue record for this book is available from the British Library

ISBN 9781529922028

Design by Nikki Dupin at Studio Nic&Lou
Photography by Andrew Hayes-Watkins
Food styling by Lola Milne
Prop styling by Rachel Vere

Colour origination by Altaimage Ltd
Printed and bound in Italy by LEGO SpA

The authorised representative in the EEA is Penguin Random House Ireland, Morrison
Chambers, 32 Nassau Street, Dublin D02 YH68.

Penguin Random House is committed to a sustainable future for our business,
our readers and our planet. This book is made from Forest Stewardship Council®
certified paper.